This

Achieve Total Quality

David Hutchins

Published in association with the Institute of Directors
DIRECTOR BOOKS

Published by Director Books,
an imprint of Fitzwilliam Publishing Limited,
Simon & Schuster International Group,
Fitzwilliam House, 32 Trumpington Street,
Cambridge CB2 1QY, England

First published 1992

British Library Cataloguing in Publication Data

Hutchins, David
Achieve total quality.
I. Title
658.5
ISBN 1–870555–38–4

Library of Congress Cataloging-in-Publication Data

Hutchins, David C.
Achieve total quality / David Hutchins.
p. cm.
Includes index.
ISBN 0–13–006057–7
1. Total quality management, I. Title.
HD62, 15, H88 1991
658.5' 61—dc20   91–27491
                                                              CIP

Distributed in the United States by Prentice Hall
ISBN: 0–13–006057–7

Designed by Geoff Green
Typeset by The Midlands Book Typesetting Company
Printed in Great Britain by BPCC Wheatons Ltd, Exeter

Contents

Preface

The object of this text is to provide the reader with a comprehensive understanding of the key concepts related to Total Quality. The book is not exhaustive on any one aspect of Total Quality, since the subject is so complex that to achieve this would require several volumes. And indeed, this is not my purpose here. Rather, the aim is to provide the busy executive with the basic knowledge necessary to avoid going down false trails in the quest for the best strategy for the company's development.

All the techniques and concepts described in this book have been tried and tested: it contains no unproven theories or hypotheses. And to support the argument, extensive use is made of case study material.

Thanks are due to the work and support of many colleagues in the writing of this book. Of particular importance are the contributions of colleagues from David Hutchins Associates Limited and the knowledge I have gained from Dr J.M. Juran. There is also the subconscious transmutation of other people's ideas, but the reader will find enough original material here to ensure that this text is a genuine contribution to this fascinating and fast-developing subject.

I stumbled unwittingly into the world of quality in the mid-1960s. At that time, I was a production engineer in an automotive component manufacturing company. The level of defects there was unacceptably high, and it was obvious that the cost of poor quality could not be sustained. To remedy the problem I introduced statistical quality control. I had learned it as a student and believed that every company except ours used it. Two decades later I realized that we had probably been pioneers in the field, even though the techniques had been invented in the 1930s. It is ironic to note the current 'discovery' of what is now referred to as Statistical Process Control, bearing in mind what we did so many years ago. However, I do not wish to take credit away from my boss at that time, Brian Banfield. Without his foresight and inspiration my career would probably have taken a different path. For, having entered the world of quality from outside the quality profession, I have been early in the field of challenging some of the basic tenets of traditional western thinking on quality. One thing is certainly true: from the first publicity related to the British Defence Standards, which came into force in June 1972 and proved to be the forerunner of BS 5750 (ISO 9000), I have never been comfortable with the principle of third party assessment. I have always believed that third party assessment leads to quality being perceived as a policing activity, parallel to operations but not intrinsic to them. Nothing that has happened since then has altered my view. It was this concern that led me to study Japanese quality before many others, and I am convinced that, in the end, Total Quality, based on project by project improvement and supported by policy management, will prevail over all other initiatives.

I should also like to acknowledge my good friend, the late Dr William Thoday, past President of the European Organization for Quality Control, who did so much to help me early in my career. The same is true for many others: the late Professor Kaoru Ishikawa, who was generous with his help, particularly in the early days of my career; many other Japanese friends now too numerous to mention, but including Mr Jonji Noguchi, Managing Director of the Japanese Union of Scientists and Engineers (JUSE); Professor Naoto Sasaki, without whose acquaintance, in 1978, I would not have learned from Professor Ishikawa; Dr Yoshio Kondo, who provided a deeper understanding of Japanese quality concepts; and Dr Noriaki Kano, who became my first Japanese acquaintance, in 1974, and who aroused such interest in Japan that it stimulated my desire to conduct more serious research.

Many readers of my generation probably still find it difficult to reconcile the extraordinary changes which have taken place in Japan since World War II. It is not so many years ago that most business people would have thought it inconceivable that Japan would hold such a dominant position in the world economy. I remember, even as recently as 1972, a respected management scientist friend of mine, Tony Shaw, saying that in a few years Japan would dominate the world economically. But even I could not believe it at the time. Now there is a generation of people in their twenties and thirties who can remember nothing but the present status quo. This book like many others makes continuous references to Japan, but Japan is no longer alone. There are other countries such as Singapore that are coming up on the fast track (see Appendix II). I only hope that through this text, the ever-expanding subject of 'quality' will give as much pleasure and satisfaction to others as it has to me, and if this text stimulates others then the effort will have been worthwhile.

Introduction

During the past four to five years the term Total Quality has become a major subject for discussion in board rooms throughout the world. Conference halls are often packed when the topic is on the agenda and, as with all fashionable management subjects, Total Quality has become an essential item on the menus of offerings by management consultants almost regardless of whether or not they can offer genuine expertise. Inevitably, as with religion, there are those who would attempt to persuade the hapless pilgrim down almost any path, many of which lead nowhere.

This book is an attempt to help business directors avoid these false trails in their quest for knowledge and enable them to gain a rapid insight into what is, in fact, a highly complex and broad subject. Total Quality was not dreamed up in someone's bath tub; it evolved over two or three decades. Much of that development took place in Japan, but the basic concepts did not originate there. Many of the fundamental ideas originated either in the United States or Europe. However, it was, in the end, the Japanese reflection of western-style management philosophy and its employee relationships which sparked the origins of Total Quality.

The book is designed to take the busy director through a logical process beginning with the definition of Total Quality through to advice on implementation.

Chapter 1, entitled 'What is Total Quality', deals with the definitions of Quality and Total Quality. The role of the consultant is also discussed, and there is an explanation of some key quality-related concepts leading to the identification of the four elements of Total Quality.

The second chapter highlights the financial benefits of Total Quality, which can be very substantial for both manufacturing and service-based organizations. It is argued that quality-related savings, which are high in most types of organization, may be especially high in service organizations, because they are less visible. The chapter then deals with the fallacy that quality-related savings can be optimized; in fact, they can be continually reduced. The point is carefully illustrated that it is this form of continuous improvement, which usually also leads to product or service improvement, that puts the greatest pressure on competitors, and could in fact force them out of business if they fail to respond.

Chapters 3 and 4 illustrate some of the tangible benefits of Total Quality, and discuss the relevant techniques using case study examples from organizations that have used Total Quality to gain competitive advantage. Examples are taken from both service and manufacturing organizations to highlight key Total Quality concepts.

Decision-making based upon fact rather than opinion is fundamental to Total Quality and this issue is dealt with in Chapter 5. Data collection and analysis, particularly when referred to as 'statistics', is often regarded as a tough subject; but simplicity is the essence of Total Quality, and this chapter is designed to show how the power of statistical analysis can be used right through the workforce through the skilful application of some fundamental concepts.

One of the objectives of Total Quality is to harness the resources of all the labour force to work towards making and keeping the business in the forefront of its marketplace. Chapter 6 analyzes some of the problems that can be experienced in achieving the goal, and illustrates how the concepts of Total Quality may be used to release this largely untapped energy.

Without good systems and procedures, an organization can easily run into all kinds of trouble, and most do from time to time. A guide to the establishment of systems of organization is contained in British Standard 5750, which is the British version of International Standard ISO 9000, and its many copies from different countries around the world. However, there has developed a strong methodology for the implementation of these standards which is not always as beneficial to the user as may appear. Chapter 7 reveals both the light and dark sides of these standards, and is intended to set them in the context of Total Quality. It should be interesting to the reader to note the Japanese attitude to this approach.

Project by project quality improvement is identified by many as the heart of Total Quality. This may or may not be true, but there can be no doubt that Total Quality could not operate in an organization without a structured programme of incremental improvement activities. Chapter 8 deals with this subject in some depth, and looks at the means by which projects are selected, how they are tackled, and how the gains may be maintained.

The final chapter deals with the implementation process and contains essential guidance for executives determined to enable the benefits of Total Quality to be obtained and the pitfalls avoided. There is sufficient information contained in this chapter to assist with the development of a strategy and to assess the suitability of would-be consultants.

Included also are two appendices which provide further dimensions to Total Quality, and also a Total Quality self-assessment health check. It should provide valuable insight to those who would like to know the current position of their own organization against world class competition. As a rough guide, such organizations would probably achieve around 70 per cent of the total possible marks!

1 What is Total Quality?

> Good business, which in turn means general prosperity and employment, is not something which comes about by chance. It is a result of the skill with which business in general is managed – and business in general is only the sum of the activities of the business units. Through all the years that I have been in business I have never yet found our business bad as a result of any outside force. It has always been due to some defect in our own company, and whenever we located and repaired that defect our business became good again – regardless of what anybody else may be doing.
>
> Henry Ford

This chapter covers:

- What the term quality means to manufactured and service products
- How it applies to the competitive concept of Total Quality
- The role of the consultant as an adviser
- Succinct definitions of the terms used in this book
- The four elements of Total Quality

At least 20p in the pound is wasted on poor quality in one form or another. This means that over 20 per cent of sales revenue of any size of company is wasted. It follows that quality-related costs amount to a minimum of 20 per cent of GNP and therefore exceed either the income from VAT or the cost of the defence budget. If these losses could be recovered, the effect on the national economy would be stunning. That is the potential of Total Quality.

Not only can costs be reduced, but profitability, productivity and saleability can be increased in equal proportion. This is what has happened in Japan, and there is no reason why the same cannot be achieved in other countries. There is nothing mysterious about Total Quality. It is not culturally specific; the concepts need no passport. Total Quality is pure pragmatism. This book is based on over twenty-five years of research into best practices, of becoming and being the best. What has come to light is phenomenal. Total Quality is a unique concept in as much as it is not a technique or a tool, it is not simply a mechanistic approach, nor is it a behavioural concept or a philosophical approach to life. It is all of these combined. Total Quality represents a totally new approach to industrial organization and to the work ethic. Total Quality challenges all forms of performance and industrial relationships. Total Quality represents an approach that is dramatically opposed to the turgid, hierarchical, blame-led, conflict-ridden industrial cultures of the past and present. Total Quality represents both a social revolution in the workplace and a rigorously effective approach to professionalism and success. The true Total Quality organization will eliminate all competition other than from other Total Quality giants. The power of a Total Quality organization is irresistible and all organizations that do not take up the challenge will die. Many have done so already. The British motor cycle industry, television industry, consumer electronics, machine tools have all fallen before the juggernaut of a Total Quality economy. Those that remain can either wait to die or respond to the challenge. For it is not too late; success is still achievable. American, British and other European companies are responding to the challenge and are proving to be world class competition. The concepts are just as applicable to a sole trader as they are to the multinationals. Indeed, through the application of Total Quality concepts it is possible for a one-person business to become an international giant; such is the potential of Total Quality.

The philosophy behind the concept of Total Quality is outlined here: the book is as much a 'what is' as a 'how to'. The text does not go into great depth on the specific techniques, for I believe that it is more important to gain an understanding of the objectives, the involvement, the issues, the successes and the vision. If you cannot grasp these, success is impossible. With a clear vision, everything becomes achievable.

What quality means

Quality is a subjective term which means different things to different people in different situations. *Webster's Dictionary* and the *Oxford Dictionary* both define quality as 'degree of excellence'. In addition to this definition, industrialists, academics and consultants have created a myriad of alternatives, for example: 'Fitness for use', 'Meeting the *at lowest cost.*

stated requirements of the customer, 'According to specification', 'The totality of features that meet a specific need', and so on.

All the industrial definitions are product-related and were created to determine precisely whether a particular product or service does or does not meet certain criteria. When applied in this way almost all these definitions have some merit; however, none of them is satisfactory when applied to the concept of Total Quality. 'Total Quality' embraces not only the quality of a specific product or service, but everything an organization does, might or should do to determine the opinion not only of its immediate customers or end-users, but its reputation in the community at large. Dr J. M. Juran, the American quality guru, defines the difference between Total Quality and product quality as capital Q vs small q.

When applied to industrial organizations, Total Quality is a competitive concept because it is concerned with being the 'best', where 'best' is defined by the marketplace rather than by the product or service provider. Quality, in terms of Total Quality, is a comparative concept and, contrary to the opinion of Philip Crosby, a well-known international consultant, cannot be regarded as an absolute. A customer's assessment of the quality of any organization is based on the best that customer has seen.

The customer does not know what is technically or organizationally feasible. So the key challenge to a competitive organization is to raise the expectations of the marketplace by providing goods and services at quality levels higher than those offered by the competition. As the competition inevitably responds to these challenges, the Total Quality company will continue to change these expectations, usually in directions not predicted by the competitor.

We can now see that there are two principal elements to Total Quality: a business strategic element based on customer-related information, aimed at identifying the strengths and weaknesses of the competition; and an organizational improvement element aimed at ensuring a faster rate of performance improvement in all aspects of the business than that achieved by any competitor.

The concept of Total Quality does not only apply to commercial organizations; it is applicable to any type of organization, even to individuals. Total Quality is just as relevant to a Government Department as it is to a voluntary organization, a community, a family. Of course, in these situations the competitive element does not apply, but organizational improvement does; all the underlying philosophy and many of the methods and techniques are just as applicable. Total Quality is an umbrella term which includes: everything that an organization does to determine whether its customers return to them and recommend them to others; minimizing costs through efficient and effective organization; maximizing the resources of the workforce to cooperate in making the company the best in the field; and finally, the exploitation of the weaknesses of the company's rivals. All these elements are interactive and policy-driven from the top down (see Figure 1.1). The market power of companies that have learned to structure their organizations to harness their potential is devastating, even when compared with companies that have hitherto seemed impregnable. Market leaders such as Rank Xerox and Caterpillar, which as recently as 1980 had between 90 and 100 per cent market penetration were reduced to a 40 per cent share, or less, in a matter of five years. The only way these two companies have managed to survive has been to learn and apply the concepts of Total Quality at a crash pace to avoid oblivion. Both are now fighting their way back.

Total Quality does not only apply to the multinationals; it applies to all types of organization and all sizes of company. It is equally valuable for small or medium-sized companies.

If a company is not currently feeling the force of the competition that hit Rank Xerox and Caterpillar, then it is only a matter of time before it does. When this happens, the choice is simple. Respond robustly or be eliminated. In many cases there will be no time

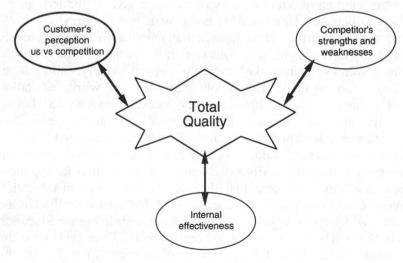

Figure 1.1 The concepts of Total Quality

to react. Rank Xerox and Caterpillar have survived because both companies invested in highly intensive reconstruction programmes. But in a significant proportion of companies, such resources are not available, or the time to react too long: in some cases, the patient will be too weak to survive the operation.

Total Quality concepts do not only apply to companies. The wealth of a country is the sum total of its wealth creation. In recent years Britain has suffered from low growth compared with its leading competitors, notably Japan. It is significant that Japan is at the forefront of Total Quality, and it is the Total Quality strategies of its leading companies which are creating the remarkable trade imbalance.

If other industrialized countries are to survive as major competitors to Japan, they must become significantly and rapidly more competitive so that customers want to buy their products because the quality and value for money they offer are the best; they cannot simply rely on patriotism. Patriotism demands that the producer supplies products and services that give pride in ownership or use. But you cannot assume that a customer will purchase an inferior national product. Protectionism only widens the gap between best and worst products due to the removal of competition. Many organizations produce *quality* products for their market but only at great cost to themselves. They are therefore vulnerable in the marketplace and lose out to those competitors that can equal the quality of their product or service but at a greatly reduced price. The gap between Japan and its main rivals is now growing so fast that nothing short of a revolution in managerial approach, vigorously driven by government, will even scratch the surface of the problem. The revolution must take place throughout society, not just in industrial companies. The whole perception of work, education and industrial relationships must be radically overhauled before any significant differences will be perceived. A senior vice-president of Milicrom, a leading US company which won the coveted 'Baldrige Award for Quality' said, 'We estimate that a typical American company must spend around 20 per cent more than its Japanese rival to achieve the same just through the difference in education levels of new entrants to the company.' If this is true for the United States, which has marginally more 16–18 year olds in higher education than Japan (United States: 79 per cent; Japan: 77 per cent) then the situation in the United Kingdom must be calamitous. For in the United Kingdom, in 1989, only 37 per cent of 16–18 year olds were in higher education. The difference between Japan and the United States lies in the differences in the *quality* of the education they offer. In the United Kingdom all the literacy and numeracy indicators suggest that its overall education is currently inferior to that in the United States on these measures. This indicates that the United Kingdom is comparatively underresourced in its stock of educated, articulate and willing new entrants to its industries. This is a serious deficiency, which is now being recognized at government level, but it will take at least a decade to right the wrongs of the past whatever action is taken. Companies must share some of this burden by running their own education programmes if they want to shorten the period.

The consultant

Many western academics, particularly those in the fields of strategic management, corporate planning and behavioural science, attempt to belittle Total Quality and describe it as nothing more than a technique or just a tool. This is generally because these academics refuse to accept the fact that Total Quality embraces their own disciplines as well as many others. Cynically, there may also be more commercial reasons for their policy. For instance, some recent authors have ascribed different terms to what is, essentially, Total Quality, thus confusing even further managers who are struggling to come to terms with all of the complexity and jargon of this important concept. The term 'lean production' has been used, for example, which implies that the concepts are related specifically to mass production industries. In fact, Total Quality applies to all kinds of industry, and all types of work, regardless of the product or service. Total Quality is a way of managing people and the organization. Some academics are probably only too well aware that to admit this would require them to undertake considerable in-depth study to at least Master's degree level across a wide range of topics if they wanted to retain their current level of credibility. On the other hand, it is surprising how many so-called Total Quality experts have sprung up in the last few years, mostly unknown in the profession, especially when you recall that the opportunities to become expert through university courses is limited in the extreme!

In addition to these 'experts', there are a number of others who, because they may be experts in some specialist but narrow areas of the subject, have convinced themselves that they must also be experts in other areas by virtue of nothing other than the acquisition of a wide specialist vocabulary. For example, some may be experts in, say, Failure Mode and Effect Analysis, or Statistical Process Control, or BS 5750. This may keep them in employment, but it does little for the credibility of the subject or for the organization which in blind faith follows their advice. Companies attempting to grasp the full meaning of Total Quality and take advantage of its potential would do well to be wary of such dubious sources of information. There are probably more failures due to wrong or inadequate consultancy advice than for any other reason. Also, do not assume that simply because a consulting company has acquired a good reputation in one field, they will necessarily be experts in another. This is particularly true of accountancy. The assumption is not borne out by the evidence. Despite impressions to the contrary, times are often hard in general consultancy, and Total Quality seems a good business to be in. These days there are few consultancies which have resisted the temptation to offer Total Quality assistance. Check every consultancy with their clients before taking any advice and do not be influenced by a consultancy's criticism of its competitors. Many of them are better at doing this than doing the work they claim to be able to perform. They are as much in competition in their field as the client company is in its own. Consultants are often experts at damning their competitors with faint praise! This is a serious problem both for industry as a whole and for the organization concerned. That is why I have raised it at such an early point in the book. It is impossible to gain anything other than a superficial understanding of the wide-ranging aspects of the subject without having spent many years of serious study across a broad spectrum of topics, or, as an industrialist, having been directly involved in the implementation of Total Quality in one's own organization. Plausible sounding 'experts' do a serious disservice to society and to industry because they debase what is probably the most important business concept to have emerged since the dawn of the industrial revolution.

Consider, for example, Quality Control Circles. In many people's eyes these have been discredited. Why? Is it because QC Circles do not work? No, they do work and have been working in the United Kingdom, the United States and throughout continental Europe since the late 1970s. The disillusionment is based on the fact that probably as many as 90 per cent of all western attempts to implement QC Circles have failed. This appalling statistic has nothing whatsoever to do with the concept itself, but everything to do with the quality of the advice given to the would-be host organization, or to the level of internal support given by upper management. Unless the key opinion-formers and decision-makers in industry accept this fact, then precisely the same fate will befall Total Quality.

Defining the terms

The *Webster's* and the *Oxford Dictionary* definitions of quality have already been given, but in the context of Total Quality, the definition given in *Roget's Thesaurus* applies namely 'A level of superiority that is unusually high'. This does not imply perfection, because to over-specify would incur unnecessary costs, which would in turn impact adversely on either selling price, cost, profit or market share. 'Superiority' in the context of Total Quality applies as much to these parameters as it does to product or service features. The challenge of Total Quality is to attempt to achieve all these features simultaneously.

Total Quality

Total Quality can best be described as 'everything that an organization, a society or a community does, which in the eyes of others determines its reputation on a comparative basis with the best alternatives'. Note that the organization can be:

1. An industrial company in any sector – manufacturing or service.
2. The industry itself, if compared with the same industry in a different country.
3. Manufacturing industry collectively, in a given country or group of countries, e.g. United Kingdom *vs* the rest of Europe, or perhaps Europe *vs* Japan. Similarly, service industries.
4. Public sector organizations on a similar basis.
5. Institutions.
6. Voluntary bodies and charities.
7. A community, or even an entire nation.

Total Quality Management

This is a sub-element of Total Quality and embraces the managerial and organizational features. It does not include the philosophical or business strategic issues. The word 'management' means 'authoritative control over the affairs of others' or 'an act or instance of guiding' or 'the careful guarding of an asset'. The addition of the word 'management' is, in the opinion of the author, unhelpful, and while it may appeal to a few egos, it does nothing to help or encourage the cascade of quality responsibility down through to the workforce.

Total Quality Control ⟵‑ع/٢/

This is the term used in Japan which translates as Total Quality, as described in this book. It is a profound concept and goes far beyond the parameters of Total Quality Management. The word 'control' implies that there is:

- A plan.
- Performance of the plan – doing.
- Comparison between plan and performance – checking.
- Corrective action on the difference.

The plan in the context of Total Quality will be a nesting series of plans, which start with a macro-plan for the whole organization, followed by a cascade of sub-plans, which extend right down, in the case of business organization, to the direct employees as autonomous groups, self-supervising work groups, and to individuals.

In the West, when used as a noun, the word 'control' has restrictive and authoritarian connotations, and its use, therefore, is not generally favoured. For this reason the simple term 'Total Quality' is preferred.

Total Quality implies the use of a disciplined and structured approach to project by project improvement activities, on a company or organization-wide basis. Project by project improvement activities are an essential element of Total Quality, where the goal is to achieve a faster rate of improvement than any competitor or rival. Phenomenal rates of improvement are being achieved by this means in organizations all over the world. As Dr Juran, one of the Total Quality pioneers, commented, the fact that an organization is improving is irrelevant if its competitor is improving at a faster rate. Therefore, it is the rate of improvement which is the critical factor.

In Figure 1.2 Company A's performance has improved, but Company B, which may be inferior to start with, is improving at a faster rate. It is only a matter of time before the two lines converge. At this point Company A is heading for trouble, and if it is unable to make up the difference, may not survive.

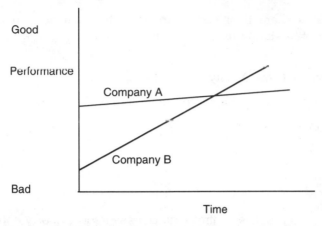

Figure 1.2   Comparative rates of improvement of two companies

Competitive benchmarking

National and international quality awards, such as the American Baldrige Award for Quality, place considerable emphasis on the need to make inter-firm comparisons on a spectrum of performance-related criteria. These comparisons may be either within an industrial sector or against 'best practice', irrespective of the industry concerned. An example of within-industry comparison might be, for example, the fact that Toyota are known to be able to change the body-stamping dies in their major plants in around two minutes. Nissan can do the same. For that particular activity, this is regarded as 'best in class', and becomes a target for all serious competitors. Of course, this particular example is specific to the automotive industry, but many such comparisons can be made across a spectrum of industries. One such example could be die changing in injection moulding. It is known that the leading Japanese companies doing injection moulding can change dies in five to eight minutes. In the West it may take as long as an entire shift.

Such comparisons can be made in almost any measure, many of which are not industry specific; for example, debtor/creditor ratios, credit period, labour turnover, age of employees, training levels, plant availability and efficiency. These comparisons have recently become popularly known as competitive benchmarking and this is rapidly becoming a major feature in Total Quality programmes. In some cases benchmarking clubs are being formed, in which participants share their secrets in order to learn how to improve to world class standards.

Elements of Total Quality

There are four key elements to Total Quality (See Figure 1.3):

1. Systems.
2. Process control.
3. Management.
4. People.

Systems and process control – quality assurance, quality control and inspection

The most important objective is to establish systems and procedures throughout the organization, which enable the identification, monitoring and eventual elimination of product-related deficiencies. Quality assurance, quality control and inspection relate specifically to the product or service being sold. If the term 'Total Quality Management', referred to earlier and which is also product-related, is being used, these concepts collectively may be regarded as its principal sub-elements.

Quality assurance is concerned with the establishment and maintenance of documented procedures designed to ensure that design, development and operational activities result in products or services

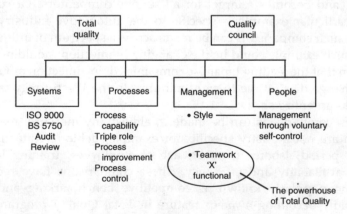

Figure 1.3 The four elements of Total Quality

which meet the customer's stated or contracted requirements. The International Standards Organization publications (the ISO 9000 series), the European Community EN 29000 series, British Standards 5750 series, and similar documents published in many countries outline the basic requirements of such procedures (See Chapter 7). Quality control, on the other hand, embraces all activities concerned with measurements, data collection and analysis, conducted within the plans laid down by quality assurance which are designed to give early warning of negative trends in processes to enable corrective action to be taken before defective work is produced.

Statistical quality control and statistical process control are both part of quality control, and include a wide range of techniques, from the simple through to the very sophisticated, for the diagnosis, elimination and control of process-related problems.

Inspection is often confused with quality control since both involve taking measurements. The fundamental difference between these two activities lies in the fact that whereas quality control takes place before the event and is a preventive activity, inspection takes place after the event. In an ideal world, inspection should not be necessary, and the goal should always be to minimize the need for inspection through the continuous improvement of processes. However, we do not live in an ideal world, and inspection as a business activity will probably be with us for a long time to come. Even in those cases where there is near-total confidence concerning defect-free products, concerns about human and environmental safety will ensure that there will always be instances where some form of statutory inspection will be needed.

It should always be remembered that inspection adds nothing to the value of a product or service. It does not matter how much you inspect a bad product, it will not make it any better; and all inspection does to a good product is to add to its cost. Better to make it right in the first place and reduce reliance on inspection.

This has led to some interesting observations regarding organizations which have introduced the concepts of Total Quality. In the past, and even today, in organizations which are introducing Total Quality Management quality is seen as a means to reduce deficiencies only, often using such dubious slogans as 'right first time' or 'zero defects'. While significant reductions in defects far beyond anything achieved by more conventional quality practices are being achieved using the broader range of techniques of Total Quality, even more significant is the impact on the time it takes to perform the various task requirements of the operation. Here results have been phenomenal. Manufacturing lead times have been reduced sometimes from months to days, or from weeks to hours. Acknowledging this fact the chief executive officer of Hewlett Packard, John Young, commented; 'In the past we competed in units of product. In the future we will be competing in units of time.'

Management and people

Those who can only relate quality to product or service deficiencies and not to the broader issues of management will, in the near future, find themselves in serious trouble if they have not already done so. Only those who understand that the true goal of the quality-related sciences and disciplines is to create organizations in which everybody is involved in activities aimed at making their organization the best in its field, are likely to survive. The object of Total Quality is to make use of the brainpower, creativity and work experience of the entire workforce to create an unbeatable organization in its marketplace. The Total Quality organization is a global competitor because only the best is good enough.

The Total Quality company will recruit the highest calibre staff at all levels. This means the best graduates from the universities and polytechnics, and the top students from local schools. In other words, an elite, unrivalled labour force. The only way to attract this resource is to acquire a reputation second to none in both the commercial and employment markets. All the leading Japanese companies are fully aware of this, employing the best is essential to their strategy. Even in the United Kingdom, there are Japanese companies which will employ school leavers with the highest grades only, irrespective of the type of job they will be doing.

Homogeneity

The Gestalt effect (the whole is greater than the sum of the component parts) is essential to the achievement of Total Quality. In the past there were many management scientists who believed that conflict was healthy within organizations. In many companies, inter-departmental competition is still regarded as being more important than competition in the marketplace. There was also a strong body of opinion which thought, and probably still thinks, that conflict is both healthy and desirable between management and labour. Others believe there must always be a struggle for the rights of the workers. These theories must be discredited if society is to make progress. An organization in which harmony exists between management and labour, between department and department, between division and division and throughout the entire management structure, and with everyone working together for the same goals and objectives, must be in a superior position to one in which everyone is at each other's throats (see Figure 1.4).

Yet there are many examples of different divisions of the same company having followed a different approach in the introduction of Total Quality for no other reason than that they do not want to be seen to have copied the other! The rationale is that they want to experiment to find the best approach, or that the various divisions are autonomous. Autonomy is all very well where local conditions demand special consideration and for issues where local ownership is important. However, in the case of corporate policy and the very survival of the organization, the merits of such autonomy are dubious. Autonomy in this case could well be regarded as abdication of responsibility or weak direction.

As far as the argument that each division should be allowed to experiment to find the best approach goes, this might be justifiable, if there were no data to evaluate the relative merits of different approaches or the abilities of different consulting organizations. That is hardly the case today. Considerable data are available both on the successes of different consulting organizations and on differences in approach. One approach is certain to be better than the others, and this could have easily been predicted, given adequate study of the results at far less cost than through this fruitless form of experimentation. And what about the divisions that 'got it all wrong'? Will they be prepared to admit it? Not usually. They will probably be prepared to do anything rather than follow the path of their more successful colleagues.

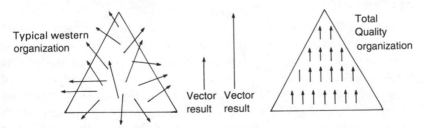

Figure 1.4   Conflict vs cooperation in a western vs Total Quality organization

There are many sources of conflict between sections of a working community; not surprisingly, they are complex. However, some of the concepts embraced by Total Quality have done a great deal to mitigate these problems and even in some cases eliminate them all together. This subject will be addressed in later chapters.

2 Quality-related costs

In this chapter all aspects of quality-related costs are discussed:

- Returns, repairs, scrap and service-related alternatives
- The hidden cost of poor quality
- The cost of failure appraisal and prevention

Also discussed are:

- The optimum quality fallacy
- Unnecessary perfectionism
- Accounting for quality costs

Who suffers most – service or manufacturing?

Quality-related costs include all costs and activities that do not add value. Because quality is a business strategic issue, reduction and control of the cost of poor quality should be a prerequisite of any quality-related initiative. The contents of this chapter apply equally to service and manufacturing organizations – as indeed does the rest of the book.

The majority of service industries are so called because in most cases, the service-giver does something on behalf of someone else (usually referred to as a customer or user) other than the mere shipment of goods. In service industries, as distinct from manufacturing, the customer is *part* of the process and affects the *quality* of the process. A polite customer will often receive a different quality of service from an impolite customer. The customer is present when the service is provided and observes the delivery of the service. In the case of manufactured products, the customer may not be present when the product is made, and does not directly influence its quality. In all other cases there really is no distinction from a Total Quality point of view between manufacturing industry and a service industry. In fact, in many instances, there may be more similarities between a service industry and a manufacturing industry than between two different service industries. What relationship, for example, is there between a hospital and a travel agency? Fortunately, from a Total Quality point of view, this does not matter because we are dealing with a generic subject. Only the vocabulary needs to be modified, but this is true of any two industries and not just manufacturing and the service sector. What is the hospital term which would be the equivalent to the manufacturing word 'scrap'? Or the banking equivalent to the manufacturing term, 'rework'?

In Chapter 1 I stated that the cost of poor quality was at least 20 per cent of sales revenue in commercial operations. This figure is potentially much higher in non-profit organizations, partly because there is less pressure to become efficient and also because quality-related costs are often less visible. In the case of government and other public organizations, there is also much confusion as to who the customer is, what the mission is and what the goods are. This lack of focus inevitably leads to wasted effort and high quality-related costs.

In reality, the results of quality cost audits across the entire spectrum of industry all indicate that the true cost of poor quality can be as high as 40 per cent of sales revenue – even higher in some cases. To say that quality costs are higher than 20 per cent of revenue is a safe assumption. Bearing in mind that these costs can be halved in three to five years, it is obvious that something must be done.

Most of the literature related to quality-related costs refers to manufacturing examples. This is unfortunate because the cost of poor quality in non-manufacturing situations can be much higher.

Costs which usually appear in the literature include:

- Customer returns and repairs.
- Scrapped products and components.
- Defect-related inspection.

These are usually recorded and the costs known.

In the service sector, the direct equivalents to those deficiencies are far less obvious and may not be formerly recorded or in some cases even known to those who are responsible. For example, in the travel industry, the equivalent to a customer repair or return may be booking the wrong hotel room. In many cases, this would be dealt with by the hotel staff, and it is possible that neither the hotel nor the customer will inform the travel agent of the error. Nevertheless the reputation of the agency will suffer, and consequently its market share will be lost without the agent knowing why. Equally, the agent will not have the equivalent of a returned product appearing in the profit and loss account. In the office environment the equivalent to a scrapped or reworked product may involve redoing a task, but the effect will be far less visible since there will be no visible scrapped or reworked product.

Inspection is also less visible in many service or non-manufacturing environments. In manufacturing operations, it is common practice for inspectors to be identifiable by the colour of their overalls and their job title. It is quite rare for these activities to be so formal in non-manufacturing situations, but they still occur, and possibly take up even more time as a result. In non-manufacturing situations, inspection is frequently an *ad hoc* activity carried out either by a colleague or by supervision. The time involved is not monitored, and if the work being inspected is returned to the originator to be redone or corrected, this may not be recorded either. Because these costs are less visible and therefore unlikely to be controlled, there is a tendency to ignore them, and a likelihood for such costs slowly to increase as inefficiencies creep in. An even more insidious quality deficiency, which is bound to be more prevalent in service than in manufacturing operations, is the problem of inefficient or unnecessary operations which do not add value.

Unnecessary operations in manufacture in many cases will require additional plant, and this must be justified financially. The related needs analysis is likely to include considerable research into alternative methods, particularly where high levels of capital investment are involved. In the case of service industries, apart from occasions where capital may be required for computer networking, there are far fewer occasions when such detailed methods analysis will be carried out, particularly during periods of sustained demand. Even when computer networking-type projects are involved, it does not follow that there will be any form of in-depth methods analysis.

Related to this problem is the fact that office operations frequently involve a far greater range of activities than manufacturing counterparts. A machine operator's tasks are usually precisely defined and leave little scope for variation. On the other hand, the daily activities of a secretary, travel courier, nurse, surgeon or salesperson may not be recorded, and the breakdown of time spent on each activity may not be known even to the individual concerned, other than by unreliable, subjective means. Even when timesheets are used to record time spent on various activities, it does not follow that the time was used efficiently. A secretary is unlikely to record that three hours were spent looking for a file, if the location of the file was the secretary's responsibility. It is unlikely that the event would be recorded accurately if it resulted in a reprimand for a colleague.

Timesheets are misleading for other reasons too. Solicitors and accountants frequently require their staff to use timesheets in order to bill their clients. In most cases, apart from certain office duties, virtually all of the time available – six to eight hours in the day – will be billed to clients. Staff are unlikely to record the fact that they are not always busy, as this may eventually threaten their jobs. Instead, the time will be billed. The unfortunate client may feel that the solicitor's or accountant's invoices are large for the service supplied, but even with access to the timesheets, it would not be possible to assess the efficiency of the work.

From the accountant's or solicitor's point of view, if the client pays without question, and if there is always an excess of demand over supply, then there is little incentive to do anything about it. Similar situations have applied in most service organizations, until recently. It is only when supply exceeds demand that solicitors or service departments begin to analyze their costs. They would probably then be in for a shock – as would the customer!

Supply and demand

It is an unfortunate fact that when an industry can sell everything it can produce, quality is almost the last thing it thinks about. All that matters is satisfying the demand at almost any price. In the decades that have elapsed since the service trades first emerged from their subservient heritage, almost all have experienced unprecedented and almost unabated boom periods. With the possible exception of the travel industry, which has always been fiercely competitive and prone to the occasional shock bankruptcy, there have been few threats. Professional service industries, such as banking and other financial institutions have, until the recession of 1990–91, been generally stable. The Civil Service is rock solid, and the hotel industry, apart from a short crisis due to the Gulf War, hasn't been able to grow fast enough, with new hotels springing up everywhere and others refurbished with major extensions. Hospitals have been constrained from meeting demand in the public sector, but this has largely been compensated for by the growth of private health care.

In almost all instances, the service industries have experienced a continuous surplus of demand over supply. There are now signs, however, that this could be changing. The recession in the United Kingdom of the early 1990s, coupled with the effect of government policies which require non-commercial bodies such as higher education and public authority activities to cover their costs, have combined to bring competition, uncertainty and the possibility of failure into organizations that were hitherto protected from the discipline of the marketplace. These factors have made organizations examine their structures and seek means of improving their performance. Even organizations faced with strong competition are affected, particularly when they are required to reduce costs. For them, the remedy may be more difficult because survival is a powerful motivator and the marketplace very unforgiving to those who fail to keep up. The difficulty for the public body, on the other hand, is related to the lack of competition and therefore the difficulty in focusing improvement activities.

For the competitive organization, the measure of achievement of Total Quality goals causes competitive benchmarking (see p. 13). It is determined by the customer and is related to competitive alternatives. For a public body, there may be no competitor, and therefore such a comparison is not possible.

One Department of the Environment may be able to study the practices of other Departments of the Environment around the world, but their circumstances will be different, and the demands of their customers and users will vary considerably. However, these difficulties can be overcome if the organization is prepared to focus on 'best performance' for each of its individual activities using competitive benchmarking. Benchmarking may well become the most important management concept of the decades ahead.

Quality-related cost elements

Within the scope of Total Quality, there are two classes of quality-related cost:

1. Costs related to a deficiency in the predicted performance of a prescribed system or operation.
2. Costs incurred because the system or operation itself is less than adequate.

In both cases, the consequential costs should be included. Most quality-related initiatives are concerned with the first of these categories, and are invariably focused on deficiencies in products. The

Table 2.1. Quality-related cost elements

Manufacture (typical)		Service (typical)	
Contamination	Error	Unclear data	Mistake
Wrong label	Short-circuit	Wrong label	Missed operation
Impurity	Open circuit	Wrong instruction	Forgetting
Scratches	Missing component	Unclear handwriting	Lost forms
Cracks	Wrong location	Torn documents	Mis-filed
Blowholes	Tears	Wrong codes	Keyboard errors
Corrosion	Warped	Obliterated data	Untidy work
Buckled	Weak mix	Misunderstood information	Wrong priorities
Dented	Wrong colour	Poor delivery	Communications

vocabulary in these cases often relates specifically to the features shown in Table 2.1.

When the consequential costs of these deficiencies are also added, costs can sometimes increase by orders of magnitude, but even this does not include the cost of lost market share due to the impact of lost quality reputation. That cost is unquantifiable in most cases.

If both the actual and consequential quality-related costs are included, then the product-related costs associated with poor quality can be placed in three categories:

1. Failure costs and consequential costs:
   (a) internal
   (b) external.
2. Appraisal costs.
3. Prevention costs.

Failure costs – internal

Internal failure costs includes all costs and losses due to doing again what has already been done, or repairing or modifying the result of an activity, together with the loss of use of existing resources. The consequential costs will include the effect on the balance sheet of excessive inventory and work in progress resulting from quality-related deficiencies. In service situations, the equivalent problems do not show in inventory, but are hidden in direct costs. Most inventory and so-called work in progress other than items actually being processed can be regarded as quality-related for one reason or another.

Internal failure costs include such items as:

- Reworking, redoing or repeating activities already performed because of inadequate performance at the first attempt.
- Scrapped work.
- Costs of modification resulting from previously undetected design or planning weaknesses. This cost includes the associated design or planning activity, changes to software, cost of retraining if methods are changed, and in the case of manufactured products, new jigs, fixtures and tools. Extra space in stores to accommodate replacement parts with different issue numbers. Revisions to parts lists, instruction manuals and the increased complexity of related service activities.
- Increases to inventory and work in progress due to disruptions to the smooth flow of work. Storage space.

Modifications due to poor quality design

The Ford Motor Company conducted an intensive study of its main Japanese rivals across a wide range of criteria including the cost of design changes after the vehicle had gone into production. It found that whereas Japanese companies invest more at the design and planning phases, their overall costs are substantially lower due to significantly fewer alterations both during and post-production. This difference is symptomatic in most industries and is illustrated in the case study of Matsuchita Refrigerator Company (See Chapter 3).

Failure costs – external

Using Dr Juran's terminology, these costs can be further subdivided into chronic and sporadic categories. The chronic problems include the underlying costs of warranty calls, servicing, complaints, engineers, etc. Some of the more spectacular costs may be in the sporadic category which, if they do occur, can produce catastrophic results. These will include:

- Product recall or withdrawal – remember Perrier, John West, Farleys and many examples from the automotive industry.
- Advertisements warning of safety risks due to some possible quality deficiency. These appear reasonably regularly, and have become more visible since the advent of new product liability registration.

- Adverse criticism in the media, particularly those that infer corruption or deliberate attempts to conceal or mislead the public.

The costs to Union Carbide from the Bhopal disaster, John West and Farleys with food poisoning, and Perrier with its chemical problem were all vast. Chernobyl already has its place in history, and the English nuclear plant Windscale was renamed Sellafield in an attempt to lose its bad reputation following its disaster. All of these incidents were preventable, as was the Zeebrugge ferry disaster. None of them would have occurred had the principles of Total Quality been employed. The catalogue of events leading up to the series of DC9 failures have done nothing to give confidence to the nervous air traveller.

External costs which are included in the statistics include:

- Failed product launch due to some deficiency in the product, identified and exposed by its first customers. These costs are invariably incurred when the producers of a product or service are so concerned to obtain prior franchise that they fail to prove the product prior to sales, with the result that the market inspects and tests it on their behalf. This was the case with Clive Sinclair. It was reported that there were warehouses full of customer returns resulting from weaknesses in the design of the connectors on the ZX 81 computer. Such a simple inexpensive deficiency in what was otherwise a first class product!
- Failure to achieve prior franchise with a superior product, leading to the loss of potential revenues.
- Failure to meet either the emotional or specified needs of the customer. This is usually caused by poor market research and poor competitor-related information.
- Inadequate and misdirected promotion (wrong launch time, etc.).
- Short shelf life in the care of chemical, food and pharmaceutical products, contamination, poor packaging and consequent adverse publicity.
- Customer complaints, recording and analysis of customer complaints, and the cost of running the so-called Customer Service Department (Customer Complaints Department is a more appropriate label, but is rarely used).
- Excessive after-delivery, service or maintenance support.
- Excessive costs including storage, delivery and all related administration.

Appraisal costs

Poor quality-related appraisal or monitoring activities include those activities that exist for no other reason than the likely presence of some deficiency that must be detected at the earliest opportunity. In addition to these, but not included, are those appraisal activities that prudence suggests must be carried out irrespective of the rare occurrence of the deficiency in question. This type of appraisal is prevalent in nuclear and chemical plants where the risk to life and the environment is so high that no level of hazard is acceptable no matter how rare. Since these appraisals will always be conducted, they are not included in the estimate of the cost of poor quality. Included activities embrace all those costs of inspection, testing and monitoring which are carried out for no other reason than that failures exist. In other words, if there were reasonable confidence that the cause of failure had been eliminated, then the monitoring or appraisal could be dropped.

Some costs can be eliminated by foolproofing the operation. A simple example is the computerization of accounts.

Prevention costs

These can also be divided into two categories. There are those prevention costs that may be regarded as an essential part of the process, for example, field testing, design proving, failure modes and effects analysis. Some practitioners would include these in the cost of poor quality ratios, but they are really a cost associated with good practice. The prevention costs that should be included are those that must be incurred if the current cost of failure and appraisal is to be reduced. These represent an investment in improvement and, if effective, should result in a significant reduction in the overall costs.

Cost of poor quality ratios

These ratios will vary considerably from company to company, industry to industry and from time to time, but typically the ratios shown in Figure 2.1 may be expected if the organization is not involved in a major attempt to identify, analyze and reduce these costs. These ratios will not be influenced greatly by the implementation of BS 5750/ISO 9000 (See Chapter 7), although the

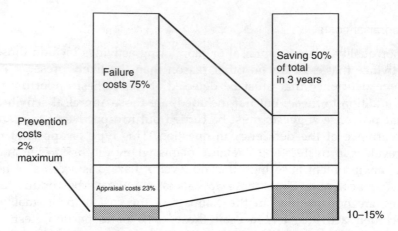

Figure 2.1   Costs of poor quality ratios

application of these standards may well reduce the likelihood of disasters such as Bhopal, Flixborough and Zeebrugge.

The main impact of BS 5750/ISO 9000 is not to reduce quality-related costs because it has no mechanism to do this, but to smooth out variations, as indicated by Figure 2.2. However, focusing on appropriate prevention activities such as project by project improvement, will reduce costs, and through the remedies applied will at the same time improve the quality systems in the places where they have biggest impact on quality (Figure 2.3).

Items that would be subject to audit according to BS 5750/ISO 9000 may not even exist in the true Total Quality organization. For example, there is the case of the ISO 9000 auditor who went to

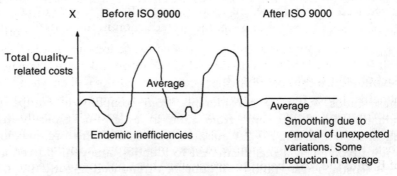

Figure 2.2   ISO 9000 and Total Quality-related costs

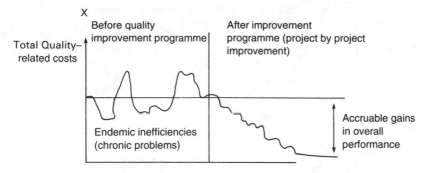

Figure 2.3   Impact of quality improvement programme

a Japanese supplier in order to make an audit. After the audit, the company asked whether he had seen everything he wanted to see. 'Well almost,' he said. 'I haven't been able to find your goods inwards stores, finished goods stores or part-finished product stores.'

'We do not have any,' he was told.

'I would also like to see the store for reject or substandard parts.'

'We don't have these either,' was the reply!

The optimum quality cost fallacy

Much of the literature on quality-related costs includes graphs similar to that shown in Figure 2.4. The theory underlying this set of curves is intended to convey the impression that there is an optimum level of quality cost, which therefore becomes the desirable target, the argument being that if a producer is at position A, then the total costs will be high due to excessive failure and appraisal costs. It is then suggested that costs will fall as more attention is given to prevention costs. However, the protagonists of this model go on to suggest that continued and progressive reductions in quality costs will eventually lead to a situation where an optimum value is reached, beyond which the cost of further prevention efforts will outweigh the benefits; hence the overall costs will rise. For example, in Figure 2.4, the company would move from position A, through position B to position C. If this were the case, then the optimization of quality costs would be a very simple matter: move from A in the direction of B until the costs begin to rise again. Then, put the brakes on, and say: 'we have achieved quality.' There is no evidence from anywhere

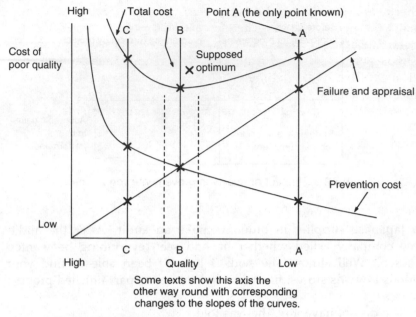

Figure 2.4 The optimum quality cost fallacy

in the world, even from Japan, that this has been achieved or even claimed. Surely, if the argument were valid, it would have happened by now!

The answer is that the argument is severely flawed. There is and can be no such optimum value. The relationship described cannot happen as described in the model because it takes no account of the relative positions of competing products or services and their influence on consumer tolerance of lower quality levels. The fact is that in the correct form of this model, the 'best' producer will always be at the optimum, irrespective of other considerations, because by definition that is what the customer wants. This is the highest level of customer expectation because the customer has no other experience. Therefore, that supplier must be at the optimum, but only until something *better* comes along, either from the supplier itself or a competitor. In all but exceptional cases, the customer only knows what he sees, and judges everything against his perceived 'best'!

We all, either consciously or unconsciously, spend our lives doing competitive benchmarking on a wide spectrum of parameters. Since we as consumers do not have the technical know-how to demand hitherto unattainable product characteristics, we judge everything against the perceived best. Therefore, it follows in the quality cost argument that the performer who has achieved the best overall mix of desirable product or service features, value for money and profitability will always be at the optimum point, and will remain there until someone else does something better, which will only be a matter of time if the currently best performer makes no improvements.

When the cost relationships are altered to include the best performer, and a less competent rival, the curve looks like Figure 2.5.

No quality absolutes!

Note the discontinuity on the failure cost curve after the point achieved by Competitor A. This is due to the fact that from the customer's viewpoint, performance levels achieved by A are also *seen* to be achievable by the customer, and therefore became an *expectation*.

Many texts on quality make the false assumption that it is the customer who identifies the required quality characteristics or specification. This is rarely the case in anything other than military or medical requirements, and even in these cases the customer must still settle for the best achievable. In general, the specification is in fact set by the 'best' performer who raises customer expectations to that level as innovation and improvement continue. By doing so, the would-be customer becomes less and less tolerant of the performance

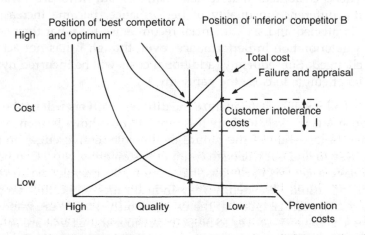

Figure 2.5 The optimum quality cost in relation to the best performer

of the inferior manufacturer even through that manufacturer's actual quality has *remained the same*.

It is evident, therefore, that *there are no absolutes where quality is concerned*. Quality is a comparative concept, and is and always will be dynamic. That is why no one has *ever* reached the optimum. It does not exist, and never can. Returning to Figure 2.5, it can be seen that the cost of failure and appraisal for competitor B has become a non-linear increase from the expected level related to competitor A. This is because a low cost element appears in both failure and appraisal costs after the point achieved by competitor A. We can call this 'customer' intolerance costs. Let us suppose that at some time in the past, competitor A performed at the same level as competitor B. At this time, the customer had seen nothing better and was therefore quite content with the service achieved, although it was obviously imperfect. The customer was therefore prepared to tolerate a wide range of deficiencies because nothing better was obtainable. Of course, there would still be costs associated with goods or services which actually failed, but these would apply equally to every one at the 'best' level. Then, competitor A makes a move and moves ahead of the competition.

Once the difference becomes known in the marketplace, two things happen:

1. Competitor A increases its share of the market at the expense of competitor B.
2. Those customers that remain with B, but who are aware of the difference in quality of performance, become increasingly dissatisfied and seek financial recompense for what they see as a deterioration in performance, even though B has not actually changed. Subsequently, additional costs will be incurred by B in its attempts to close the gap with A.

First of all B will have to analyze the differences. This will not be easy because A is unlikely to share this type of know-how. In many cases, B may be unaware of the nature of the competitive edge, and the only way to find out will be to conduct customer surveys. Companies that have done this in the past have often had unwelcome surprises from the results. Frequently they indicate that while the company may be surprisingly good at the things which it *thinks* are important to the customer, it proves to be poor at those things that are actually important to the customer. In one example known to the author, a company was losing market share but did not know why. A survey revealed that the customers did not like the company because they thought it to be both arrogant and conceited. This was a great shock to everyone in the business, and to their credit the problem was addressed.

Large differences between competitors A and B can result in many additional costs for B due to panic. These include:

- Attending conferences and seminars to try to find ways to improve and then selecting the wrong strategy. This may be repeated several times with obviously disastrous results as the gap between A and B is continuing to widen.
- Hiring consultants who are not competent to right the wrongs. This can be an expensive mistake.

Take three competitors, companies A, B and C. The quality-related costs for each are shown in Figure 2.6. It can be seen that C's intolerance costs will be higher than B's, and for any competitor worse than this, the cost will become progressively higher. There will be a point where these costs become so high that it becomes impossible to compete. Such competitors go out of business in a free market. The dynamics of this argument indicate graphically why competition is necessary for high performance. Without competition there is no incentive for the poor performer to improve. It also goes some way towards explaining why it has been such a traumatic experience for organizations in the public sector to learn to live with privatization – the rules of the game are totally different. It does not mean that the public body should

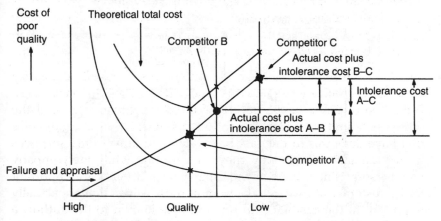

Figure 2.6 Quality-related costs of companies A, B and C

not *seek* to improve, it only means that it experiences no *pressure* to improve. It is up to governments to do something about that.

The Hutchins Hypothesis

Quality costs are optimum at the level of the 'best' performer in a given market, as perceived by the product and service user. For all inferior performers, the total cost will increase both as a direct result of the inferior performance and as a result of increasing intolerance on the part of the product- and service-user as the performance capabilities of the 'best' performer became known.

Observation

Quality-related costs can be halved in 3–5 years. In the case of the company that has quality-related costs in the region of 20 per cent of sales revenue, this will result in a minimum of 100 per cent increase in profits because the savings always go straight to the bottom line for very little increase in cost. It may also be possible to increase prices and market share because people will always be prepared to pay more for better quality (Figure 2.7).

Figure 2.7 is somewhat idealistic but indicates in principle another dimension to the quality cost curves. Of course, the argument may not apply in situations where the customer is using lowest price tender, but unfortunately, and almost invariably, such contracts will usually involve a customer who is not subject to competition. If it were otherwise, such a policy would be highly questionable. In a

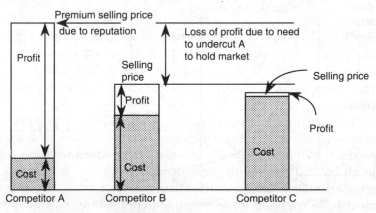

Figure 2.7 Prices and market share in relation to quality

competitive world, who would trust the reputation of their business to the performance of competitor C, whatever its selling price?

Unnecessary perfectionism

The argument thus far is based on the assumption that improvements in quality are perceived by the customer to be desirable, and that the customer is prepared to pay for them. Quality improvements that cannot be perceived by the customer, or to which the customer is indifferent and cost more to achieve, or for which the customer is not prepared to pay, must be regarded as unnecessary perfectionism. These improvements should be regarded as quality deficiencies just as much as those that relate to failure to achieve.

Sometimes unnecessary perfectionism can be one of the most significant quality-related costs.

Several years ago, one manufacturer had a near absolute monopoly of the smoke detector market. At that time, soon after clean air laws had been introduced, the company was able to sell its products at premium prices because there was no competition. However, it had also fallen into the trap of unnecessary perfectionism. The company directors insisted that the outer cases of the product were die-cast and vitreous-enamelled. These features were totally unnecessary from a practical point of view. Once installed in a chimney the customer would be indifferent as to the aesthetics of the product and much more concerned with its reliability, effectiveness and, of course, safety compatibility with related instrumentation. The aesthetic product features were included for no other reason than vanity. Because of the importance of the visual characteristics of other products in its range, the company made the false assumption that its customer expected all its products to look alike. This turned out to be an expensive mistake. When the market was at its peak, a competitor appeared. Its product was simple, functional and cheap. The overspecified product was wiped from the market at a single stroke.

The most insidious and difficult to control form of overspecification occurs in the tolerances on dimensional variation in engineering products. Only a relatively small number of dimensions on most products require tightly controlled tolerances. For most of the remainder, the designer often faces a dilemma. The dimensions must have specified limits to guide manufacture, but there are few guidelines as to what would be acceptable to the user. In such cases the designer is most likely to play safe, because, if the tolerance is too loose, the product will be inferior in some way and the designer will be blamed. However, if they are unnecessarily tight the designer is unlikely to suffer criticism because the dimension will probably not be challenged, provided that the product is manufacturable. In most instances this would be the case – but only at a price. Production engineers, production departments and inspectors will make the assumption that the designer knows best and therefore accept the specified constraints. Any items that subsequently fail to meet these requirements will either be scrapped or reworked, even though in practice they may be perfectly functional. Costs associated with such over-perfectionism must run to untold millions every year.

Accounting for quality-related costs

Total Quality begins and ends with the profit and loss account and the balance sheet. Many companies and organizations which are debating whether or not to introduce Total Quality are worried about the cost, particularly if consultants are likely to be involved. Of course, there is never an argument in favour of throwing money at a problem, and all additional costs must be weighed against the potential benefit they bring. This applies no less to quality strategies.

This is one of the drawbacks of starting a quality-led business development programme based on BS 5750/ISO 9000 (See Chapter 7). In this case, the costs are all too obvious, whereas the financial benefits, despite the claims of its principal advocates, may be obscure to say the least. Many organizations attempt to implement BS 5750/ISO 9000 before starting a Total Quality programme either because a demanding customer expects it, or because a key competitor has done so and is attempting to capitalize on the fact. In these cases, there is a very high risk that the company will introduce the standard, not because it believes in the concept but because it is forced to do so. This is the very worst reason. The company in this case will almost certainly end up with two systems, the one they show the auditor, and the one they actually use. Cynicism will be rampant, upper management will be accused of lack of quality-mindedness and suspicions will be rife. Many will be alienated from the idea of quality and see it as a surveillance activity because of preoccupation with BS 5750/ISO 9000. Any subsequent attempts to introduce Total Quality will suffer as a result. In some cases the start of Total Quality has been retarded by as much as ten years.

These problems can be overcome if BS 5750/ISO 9000 is introduced as part of a Total Quality programme and the reasons clearly stated as being to become more competitive and to lead the field. With this objective BS 5750/ISO 9000 may or may not be the first item on the agenda. In some cases, it will be due to customer or competitor pressure or perhaps to chronic weaknesses in the control of procedures. More usually it will be the former. Where then, should the competitive organization start? What should the first moves be?

The profit and loss account and balance sheet can often provide the answer, for it is here that the biggest quality costs are hidden and the best clues as to where to start can be found.

Profit and loss account

The profit and loss account contains three principal components:

1. Sales.
2. Direct cost of sales.
3. Overheads.

Consider the forecast profit and loss account for the Ace Hosiery Company for January 19XX.

Sales	£	
Fishnet stockings	X X X X	estimated by
Men's pants	X X X X	the sales
Ladies' vests	X X X X	department
Total sales		
Direct costs		
Yarn	X X X X	estimates based
Dyeing	X X X X	on historical
Labour	X X X X	costs
Total direct costs		
Gross profit		
Overheads		
Rent	X X X X	estimates based
Rates	X X X X	on historical
Heating	X X X X	costs
Administration	X X X X	
Total overheads		
Net profit before tax		

The figures for forecast sales are usually obtained from the Sales and Marketing Department. Positive variances lead to increases in finished goods stocks; negative variances produce decreases in finished stocks or potential out-of-stock situations.

Most western countries accumulate finished goods stocks, and these appear as stocks under current assets on the balance sheet. Since 'out of stock' is usually regarded as a potentially lost sale, it is treated more seriously than excess stock, with the latter frequently only regarded as a problem during a cash crisis. The result is that finished goods stocks begin to pile up. This in turn leads to stock deterioration, loss of shelf life, depreciated value and, of course, all of these have negative effects on gross profit, since the direct costs will have been incurred without any corresponding actual sale.

Remember: quality-related costs are all those costs that do not add value.

There are four primary reasons for finished goods stocks:

1. Uncertainty of demand and long lead-times.
2. Uncertainty of supply due to inefficiencies in the supply process. These will not be improved by reliance on third party BS 5750/ISO 9000 approval.
3. Slow speed of response by manufacturing facilities to changes in demand.
4. Unreliable production capability leading to stockpiling of finished goods.

Uncertainty of supply and slow speed of response are interacting problems. Both are quality-related and can only be resolved by intensive quality improvement programmes focused on processes. Theoretically, when both are brought well under control there would be no need for finished goods stocks. But this control *must* extend to suppliers, and demands first party assessment, long-term contractual relationships and considerable cooperation and trust. That is why this book is very critical of third party assessment process of BS 5750/ISO 9000. Reliance of purchasing organizations on the remoteness of this approach has seriously impeded the development of this critical aspect of Total Quality.

The major Japanese companies do not even make allowance for finished goods warehouses on their premises other than for goods that will be shipped out over the next few hours. All the major companies use first party assessment. The 'Toyota Family' (the term used by Toyota for all their key suppliers) is a prime example. The total value of finished goods stocks and the associated variances which led to their creation can be regarded as being part of the total cost of poor quality.

Direct costs

Data which enable the creation of management accounts for forecasting direct costs and overheads are usually extrapolated from historical data by the Accounts Department. The data thus prepared comprise three elements:

1. The actual cost for each item.
2. Legitimate losses in setting up.
3. The inefficiency cost for each item. This includes excessive set-up losses; excessive set-up time in efficient use of plant and equipment; excessive downtime; and poor yield from labour and materials.

The accountant has no way of distinguishing between 2 and 3, when applied to direct labour and supervision, the use of raw materials, energy and other resources. The best indicator of such costs can be obtained from zero cost budgeting, i.e., how much would it cost to operate if there were no losses? The difference between zero cost budgeting and the current actual costs represents the challenge of project by project improvement.

Experience indicates that extraordinary gains are possible. For example, Nippon Steel reduced the total energy requirement for steel-making by 40 per cent between 1973 and 1977. In 1950, when Toyota were offering poor competition to Ford, the Toyota management found that they took ten times as many workers to build a car as Ford. Today the situation has been reversed. Toyota didn't know how many workers were actually required, so they simply removed some from the assembly line. Later, they removed some more, and so on. This process forced the line managers to concentrate their attention on how to produce the same number of cars with fewer resources. As soon as they found a way, more workers were removed. What is more, none of the workers lost their jobs, they were retrained as sales people!

There is considerable evidence to support the fact that most organizations, however lean they think they are, are in fact grossly overweight, with most of the fat hidden in direct costs and overheads.

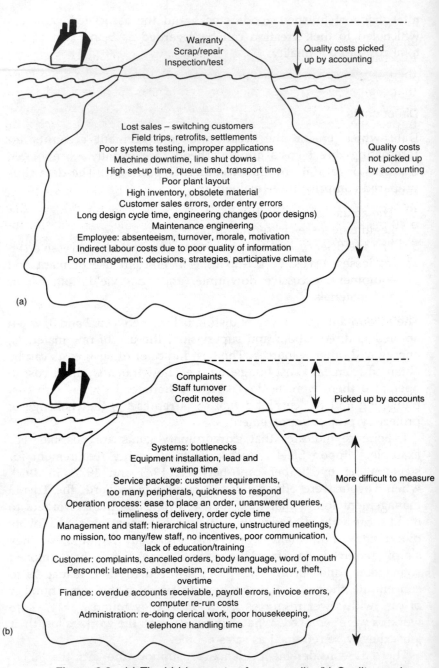

Figure 2.8 (a) The hidden costs of poor quality (b) Quality service-related costs

Usually, an overweight person will not make a serious attempt to slim unless frightened into doing so by a doctor. The same applies to organizations. It is too easy to maintain the status quo all the while there is no pressure to change. It is only in times of severe recession that companies turn their attention to this fact. Even then, unless the threat is so severe as to be life threatening, the toughest and most unpalatable decisions will often be avoided. It is amazing how lean a company can become in terms of direct costs, indirect costs and overheads before the ability to earn revenue and provide a quality service are in any way undermined. It has been observed many times that, during the three-day week caused by the early 1970s' miners' strike in Britain, total national output was unaffected. That a 40 per cent increase in production was possible even without the application of quality improvement activities gives some indication of what potentially is achievable.

Summary

1. Quality-related costs occur in all industries and in all forms of work.
2. Quality-related costs can be categorized into three elements:
    (a) failure
    (b) appraisal
    (c) prevention.
    These collectively account for over 20 per cent of sales revenue, the largest being failure costs, which normally represent 60–80 per cent of the total.
3. By identifying and tackling failure costs, the cost of poor quality can be reduced by over 50 per cent in 3–5 years. These savings represent profit.
4. Quality-related costs include the consequential cost of failure. When that is included, quality-related costs become comparable to the 'best' performer. The best performer will always be operating at the optimum value. Inferior competitors' costs will be progressively higher and will increase if the best performer improves, even though their performance remains the same – the Hutchins Hypothesis.
5. Quality-related costs due to excessive stocks of raw materials and part-finished products. Finished goods and work in progress can only be reduced through first party assessment in collaboration

with suppliers. Reliance on third party assessment schemes such as BS 5750/ISO 9000 cannot produce Total Quality performance.
6. The concept of multiple sourcing of suppliers is outmoded and must be eliminated. The 'Toyota Family' system (see p. 38) is the most promising alternative.

3 Total Quality success stories 1

This chapter examines Total Quality in practice in two service and one manufacturing industries. The case studies highlight:

- The PDCA cycle of continuous improvement
- The problem of subcontracting
- Product design and the cost of getting it wrong
- JIT or stockless production
- Employee involvement, including QC Circles

In this chapter, a number of leading Japanese examples have been selected to highlight the essence of Total Quality. These examples have been chosen because they illustrate the degree of board-level commitment essential to the achievement of the full power of Total Quality. The first is an excellent example of Total Quality in a service industry and also represents pure pragmatism and a professional and entrepreneurial approach to management. The actual results and methodology can be applied in any hotel, restaurant or night club anywhere in the world if the management has the will. The principles behind the approach are also applicable to almost any other industry, although obviously the detail would be different.

The second, which is from the same industry, is used to illustrate the management thinking typical of Total Quality and may be food for thought for some western companies faced with a similar situation.

The third example describes the impact of Total Quality on a major white goods manufacturer.

Kanzanji Hotel

The Kanzanji Hotel is situated to the south of Tokyo, adjacent to a lakeside resort, near Hammamatsu City. The hotel, which is quite large and privately owned, suffers fierce competition from a major hotel chain. The key sales comparators between the two hotels are occupancy, bookings in the restaurant, functions, night club, karaoke and shop sales. The management decided to achieve improvements in all these areas through the principles of Total Quality. Fundamental to Total Quality is the principle of project by project improvement. The scope of a project is dependent on the level within the organization. The higher the group level of participation in the organization, the broader and deeper will be the project selected. Many high-level projects break down into sub-projects and even sub-sub-projects. Each of these sub-projects may be regarded as full projects if dealt with by lower-level groups. Such was the case with the Kanzanji Hotel. Improving the overall sales revenues was a major project initiated by the top management team. However, as we shall see, sub-elements of the project were dealt with by lower-level groups, including the staff in the kitchen, hotel shop, front of house, in reception and everywhere relevant to the overall project.

In Japanese companies there is an established discipline associated with project by project improvement, which involves a stepwise approach. The first step is called 'Record the Current Situation'. At this stage information is collected to determine the extent of the problem. This discipline applies all the way through to individual and group improvement activities.

In order to effect this stage, two methods were used:

1. Extensive use of questionnaires.
2. Closed circuit television.

The objective in both instances was to provide a reference data base on the current state of customer satisfaction. It was recognized that there are two aspects to measuring customer satisfaction in a service situation: (1) tangible measures; (2) intangible or subjective measures. Tangible measures include such issues as: service too slow, room too cold, too noisy, faulty facilities, etc. These can be measured or counted, as can customer complaints. However, in all service situations there is also a complexity of intangible factors which cannot be quantified, are difficult to identify and usually result in either feelings of satisfaction, dissatisfaction or, more normally, indifference. Indifference is the most difficult to deal with because feedback is difficult to obtain. Recognizing this, the hotel management encouraged the staff to persuade customers to complete the questionnaires. These were placed in locations such as bedrooms, the restaurant and the nightclub to provide a reference data base before any changes were made.

The closed circuit television cameras were strategically placed in public areas, principally in reception and at the check-out desk. The object was to study the customers to determine their satisfaction, indifference or dissatisfaction from their facial expressions and body language.

The second stage was to identify the key process variables for each service activity. For example, in reception the variables were:

- Level of illumination at the desk.
- Design of registration form.
- Attitude of reception staff.
- Height of reception desk.
- Location of reception desk and proximity to door.
- Room tariff.

Variables in the restaurant were:

- Choice on menu.
- Price.
- Lighting.
- Ambience.
- The time to be shown to table, to be served and the time between courses.
- Crowding.
- Layout of menu.
- Wine list.
- Staff attitude.
- Quality of preparation and presentation.
- Quality of cooking and the product.

In each situation, the variables were identified, together with the means of measurement. The relative importance of each of these was compared with information obtained from the questionnaires. Changes were then made systematically with their effect measured by changes in customer reaction as recorded on the questionnaires, and in some cases by study of the closed circuit videotapes. In the case of the tapes, the customers' expressions were studied to determine any changes. This was particularly useful when the lighting was modified. In this case, the lighting was changed progressively from very dim to excessively bright on a graduated basis. Each level was measured in lux units. The video indicated the degree of comfort experienced by the customer. This was studied at reception and in the restaurant, night club and corridor areas. A similar exercise was conducted using varying levels of sound in the nightclub.

From all of these studies an enormous quantity of data was obtained. Analysis of the data resulted in many projects, sub-projects and sub-sub-projects. The Japanese Union of Scientists and Engineers (JUSE) were invited to conduct long-term monthly quality training courses for all levels of staff. Quality Control Circles were established throughout the hotel, and engineering contractors were brought in to make structural changes to the lighting, heating and layout of the hotel. JUSE consultants worked with Quality Control Circles on some of their major projects, particularly those in the kitchens.

Changes were made to the height of the reception desk, the levels of illumination, proximity to the door, the design of registration forms and the approach of the reception staff to the customer.

Nightclub

It was found that the desirable levels of lighting and sound in the nightclub varied, depending on the time of night. Early in the evening the illumination levels needed to be higher than later in the night. In the case of sound levels, these were required to increase as the evening wore on. This might have been expected, but the important factor was that not only had this been established scientifically, but the hotel knew the precise levels for each variable to obtain maximum satisfaction at all times.

Restaurant

Many useful findings resulted from this study. As with the other projects, the lighting in the restaurant was an important consideration. One surprising finding was that while customers were prepared to wait between courses, the delivery of the hors d'oeuvres was critical. In the case of a banquet when many people would require serving at the same time, this put an enormous strain on the kitchen organization. This led to three major Quality Control Circle projects. The first was to establish a faster method of hors d'oeuvre preparation. The waiters themselves designed a conveyor system with the help of an engineer. The second project was to find a way of relieving the congestion that resulted from the return to the kitchen of dirty crockery. The solution was the design of an automatic conveyor-based washing-up machine and the development of a high-powered, multi-head water jet to clean the insides of narrow-necked saki bottles on a batch basis. The third project resulted in the design of multi-layer trolleys for the transfer of the hors d'oeuvres from the kitchen to the dining room. Two different designs were introduced depending on whether the trolley was required to travel in the lift to other floors for private parties, or simply travel to the restaurant. In both cases, the trolleys required multiple wheels to spread the load and avoid damage to the rice straw tatami floor mats. The design for use in the lifts required wheels at different heights at the ends in order to negotiate variations in floor height on entering the lift.

The shop

Again, in the shop the lighting project was applicable, but an interesting improvement was introduced, which came from a Quality Control Circle. In Japan, the presentation of gifts is almost as important as the gift itself. It was found that much potential custom was lost if a lot of people wanted to check out at the same time and did not have much time to spend in the shop. In such a situation service had to be speeded up; but gift wrapping, if done properly, cannot be hurried.

The Circle came up with the novel idea of attaching the appropriate wrapping paper to the product, pre-cut to size, and in such a way as to make it easy to wrap after purchase. This saved a considerable amount of time and led to increased sales with no loss of quality.

Training

Training of middle-band managers became an ongoing monthly activity. This was coordinated by a quality executive. This person was responsible for ensuring the smooth operation of the overall programme and for liaising with both the JUSE instructor and the various consultant engineers. The training conducted by the JUSE counsellor included all the principles of Total Quality, quality-related costing, project by project improvement skills, statistical analysis techniques and organizational theories, and the continuous development of method study techniques and problem-solving tools.

Training for direct employees was different. Generally, in Japan, hotel work is not attractive to academic high-fliers, and it was thought unlikely that kitchen staff, room service personnel, etc. would gain from traditional teaching methods. The training had to be fun and socially interactive in order to develop team work and team skills, while at the same time introducing the problem-solving techniques in a non-threatening way and using a medium acceptable to the non-academic worker. The management of the Kanzanji Hotel decided to use an out-of-door approach based on orienteering principles and referred to as a 'walking rally'. Participants were divided into teams, and each team was required to navigate a course given a map, some clues and a compass. The course was designed to make use of all of the basic Quality Control Circle problem-solving skills and was competitive, with points being awarded for a variety of criteria, including the effective use of the skills, teamwork, innovation, etc. These courses were very successful and eventually all direct employees were exposed to the method.

Hawaiian Spa

The Hawaiian Spa is a health and leisure centre in the proximity of Tokyo and the first business of its kind to win the coveted Deming Award (see Appendix II, p. 182). Prior to becoming a health spa, the business was a private coal mine which was reaching exhaustion; and here is a lesson for some western business people. The owner of the mine had a strong sense of responsibility to the workers and their families. As a community, they had lived and worked together for generations, just like in the mining districts in Britain. The owner took a break in Hawaii in order to meditate and think about what could be done to preserve the community. Hawaii is noted for its spa resorts, which are popular with the Japanese, and it occurred to him that he could create something similar in the vicinity of the mine, since the mine was in an area of geothermal activity and surrounded by mountains.

On his return, he put his idea to the community, who responded enthusiastically. The mine was closed, and the site redeveloped into a spa resort. During this time the miners, their wives and families underwent extensive retraining as waiters, waitresses, receptionists, fitness training specialists and all of the other tasks required. Following this, extensive quality training was given at all levels.

The spa was a huge success. And eventually its quality achievements became such that it qualified for the Deming Award.

It makes one wonder what might be achieved in the beautiful valleys of south Wales and parts of Northumberland where whole communities are being devastated by the loss of their livelihood and the heritage of generations as the coal mines are closed.

Matsuchita Refrigerator Company

The plant is situated in the Shiga Prefecture at Kusatsu near Kyoto. Virtually all kinds of domestic refrigerator/freezers, freezers, refrigerators, computer-organized refrigerators and freezers are made in this division of Matsuchita Electric. The plant has 1,400 employees, with a total site space of 128,000 m² and floor space of 10,300 m² with a productive capacity of 3,100 standard six units (3,002,400 litres) per day and 600 compact units (502,110 litres). This plant, together with a sister plant at Fujisawa, account for 25 per cent of the domestic market (Hitachi and Toshiba each have 16 per cent and Sanyo and Sharp have around 10 per cent each).

The total demand is stable, at around 4.46 million units per year. The demand, however, is sliding into the compact refrigerators on one hand, due to the fact that in Japan the number of people remaining unmarried is increasing, and also there is a growing tendency for people to own more than one fridge; and large models on the other, because of diversification in eating habits, and the tendency to buy foodstuffs in bulk at supermarkets. Also, trade liberalization has led to increased imports of meat. A further factor has been a change in the use of kitchen space resulting from the purchase of system kitchens, as in the West.

As with major Japanese companies, the performance of this plant is impressive by any standard. The company has introduced and continually develops a highly visible Total Quality-driven culture. The seven basic features of Total Quality, which are displayed around the plant and in the reception area, are typical of those found throughout Japan, and are shown in Table 3.1.

1. All participate and all play main roles: In the next chapter, the full meaning of this concept will be explained in detail. Briefly, in Japan, Total Quality means that it is only through the total involvement of everyone at all levels from the top to the bottom of an organization that success can be achieved in a competitive market. The object is to maximize everyone's creativity and job knowledge to make their company the best in the field. This is much much more than a pious hope. The achievement of this objective is recognized as being one of the primary responsibilities of upper management.

2. Quality first: Evidence of the importance given to this objective can

Table 3.1. Basic concept of Total Quality Control at Matsuchita Refrigeration Company

1.	All participate and all play main roles	Participative management and activities with company-wide collective wisdom and capabilities.
2.	Quality first	Give the highest priority to Quality improvement and aim to secure profit by achieving superior quality of products.
3.	Repeat PDCA cycle	Strictly stick to PDCA cycle in order to achieve all QC activities effectively and efficiently.
4.	Customer-first principle	Manufacture the products and give services considering the customers' satisfaction and usability.
5.	The next processes are our customers	Proceed your works considering that the genuine customers are the recipients of 'goods and service' created by your process.
6.	Facts control	Manage and control all your jobs based on fact. Do not rely on experience and sense.
7.	Respect humanity	The basic theory of TQC is to respect humanity, and to develop fully characteristics and abilities as a human being.

be found everywhere throughout the organization – not in the form of uninspired, commercially produced posters, which make little impact on anyone, but through the display of quality information and active project work.

3. Repeat PDCA cycle: The PDCA cycle is fundamental to Japanese Quality Control, and is a development of the closed feedback loop more usually associated with the servo-mechanisms of electro-mechanical process control.

PDCA stands for PLAN–DO–CHECK–ACTION. The concept of the feedback loop as applied to Quality Control was first conceived by Dr Walter Shewhart in the 1930s. It was communicated to the Japanese in 1950 by Dr Edwards Deming in the form PLAN–DO–ACT. The Japanese subsequently developed it into its current form of verb, verb, verb, noun.

Plan – to form a strategy for
Do – to begin and carry through to completion

Check – to subject to a procedure that ascertains effectiveness, value, proper function
Action – something done

The application of PDCA is continuous and, conceptually, can be seen to rotate like a wheel. The concept is often referred to as 'The Deming Wheel' (Figure 3.1). 'Plan' occurs at all levels of organization from the bottom right through to the top. At the top the 'plan' is macro and applies to the whole organization. At each level down, the plan becomes more and more parochial until, at the bottom, the work groups create micro-'plans' for their own activities. The nesting of these plans is called 'policy deployment' and is explained in Chapter 9.

4. Customer-first principle: 'Market in/product out' is more than a slogan in Japanese companies. It is all too easy for anyone, in any specialist field, to be product-minded rather than market-minded and so focus too much on specific technical product features and give insufficient attention to non-technical aspects, which in some cases may be at least as important from the customer's point of view. In the United Kingdom, some companies have commissioned consultants to conduct customer surveys on their behalf. In almost every case, the results have come as a shock to the directors. The criticisms covered aspects of service which the company had not even considered, and had therefore never measured.

Customer information in Japanese companies is used not only to ensure the best product features; it is used to gain a position

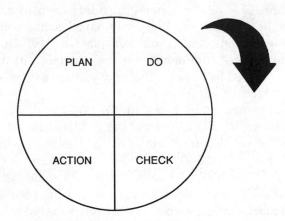

Figure 3.1   PDCA – the Deming Wheel

of superiority over the competition. Japanese companies such as Matsuchita are constantly moving the goalposts away from the competition by changing customer expectations towards features they believe to be one of their core strengths but a weakness in their competitor.

5. The next processes are our customers: In the West this is referred to as the 'triple role' and is based on the observation that each individual in an organization at any level is part of a process. Simultaneously, they are processors, customers from an upstream activity and suppliers to someone downstream. This is true for both individuals and departments. As far as can be ascertained, the concept of internal customer/supplier was first identified by Professor Ishikawa. While many western companies are now very aware of the concept, many Japanese companies now have some 20–30 years of development in reducing the problems that occur at the customer/supplier interface. This subject will be treated in more depth in Chapter 8.

6. Facts control: This is the single most important contribution to the post-war reconstruction of Japanese industry attributed to Dr Edwards Deming. A powerful and forthright speaker, Dr Deming left the Japanese in no doubt about the importance of decision-making based on fact. Fundamentally, this was one of the key pillars of the Deming Award, and a principal and significant difference between Japanese and western managements.

The reasons why Japanese organizations respond more readily to the collection and analysis of data are debated and debatable. Some believe it is due to cultural differences, but others believe it is one of the features of a new engineering society keen to excel and to do things right, whereas the West may have become soft and lazy. Whatever the reasons, the results are plain to see. One eminent Japanese industrialist commented on the reluctance in the West to respond to this need by saying: 'Probably you are not yet sufficiently frightened to face up to this fact!'

7. Respect humanity: Many people in the West think this is the sole basis of Japanese Total Quality, and yet in Matsuchita Refrigerators it is only one of seven criteria. However, it does tie in with all of the others. Each person is the expert at his or her job, and is expected to work willingly. This may take some doing with some tasks, but it is a challenge the Japanese fully accept. At Matsuchita, self-assessment schemes, Quality Control Circles and a lively suggestion scheme are all evidence of the application of this requirement.

Subcontracting

Virtually all components are internally produced in order to assure consistent quality. This is quite different from western companies, which subcontract at least 50 per cent of component manufacture. Western companies also use more than one supplier, using BS 5750/ISO 9000 as their only control. They get what they deserve! Consequently supplier quality control is often a tremendous problem. There is also a tendency for large Supplier Quality Assurance and Purchasing Departments. Vendor control and parts storage become a major factor on the balance sheet under the heading 'Stocks'.

Automation

In common with a great many major Japanese companies, there is far less evidence of automation than many westerners would expect. In fact, despite the fact that 1,900 units per day are produced, approximately 90 per cent of the work is done by hand and only 10 per cent automated. However, virtually all cabinet production is automated. This includes blanking, piercing, polishing, bending and spot welding. Die changing takes an average of 36 seconds! This would compare with several hours in some western companies.

The daily production target is based on 100 per cent uptime and currently only 10 minutes per day on average is lost. In contrast, it is widely accepted in the West that 80 per cent plant utilization is optimal; this is based on queuing theory derived from operational research. The theory is based on the statistical Poisson distribution of random arrivals under which it can be shown that with random arrivals, or random interruptions, alarming delays or queues can form once intensity of utilization extends beyond 80 per cent. Mathematically, the theory is correct, and its application witnessed everyday by motorway travellers in the most densely populated areas. Leading Japanese companies have completely disproved the effects of this theory through the almost total avoidance of interruptions. This would be extraordinary enough on a highly predictable, single-product line. The fact that all models are made on the same assembly line, and mixed in a random pattern based on demand, is nothing short of amazing. To the visitor, walking along the line with no knowledge of these factors, there would appear to be nothing out of the ordinary. It is questionable how much – apart from observing the almost clinical cleanliness – the casual observer would gain from such an experience. To the informed visitor, the achievement is stunning.

For another example of these incredibly high plant utilization figures, let us look at ASMO, a manufacturer of small electric motors for the automobile industry, which produces a range of over forty different motors on the same assembly line and achieves 96 per cent uptime on the entire operation, consistently every day.

Product design

Seminars on new product design are among the most poorly attended of all management topics in the United Kingdom, and this has constantly been the case for more than three decades, possibly more. This apparent lack of interest is also reflected in textbooks and comparisons between Japan and the West. Rarely is there any comment on differences in this area. This blind spot reflects what is probably the worst level of ignorance and misplaced complacency on the part of westerners with regard to Japan's competitive edge. In the West there is an almost universal belief that westerners are innovators and the Japanese merely copiers. Today, the only copiers which can be found in Japan are those produced by Canon and Ricoh. It is years since the Japanese woke up to the fact that they could no longer copy the West because they were already ahead. This fact dawned on the Japanese years after the cross-over had occurred and is well illustrated in the case of Matsuchita, where a major product remodelling or upgrade takes approximately 12–15 months compared with one year for a typical western competitor. However, this timescale is the only area where Japanese inferiority persists. Following product launch, it typically takes the company two weeks to achieve > 99 per cent defect-free production, no rework and no customer returns. This compares with a typical western equivalent of 40 per cent defect-free two years after product launch, at about the time when the next major uplift is due. Furthermore, the western manufacturers will also experience 40 per cent customer returns on first submission. The cost differences between these two situations is colossal.

In the late 1970s the Ford Motor Company conducted a study in which it compared the cost of engineering changes both during and following product launch between themselves, Mazda and Toyota. Figure 3.2 shows the results.

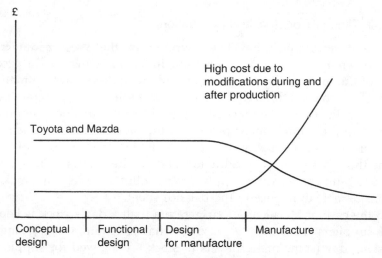

Figure 3.2   Cost of engineering change notes

Ford's results are typical of a great many western manufacturers in the 1990s. In fact, it is unlikely that the situation has changed at all in the past decade. Why? Because, as was noted earlier, the western manufacturer is unaware of these differences. In the case of Ford it is different. Ford have made impressive improvements over the past decade, because it took the trouble to collect the data.

While the data from Matsuchita Refrigerators are startling, the fact that product development takes longer than the western equivalent is not the answer to the difference in performance because this difference is not typical of Japanese companies as a whole where similar defect-free results may also be obtained. More usually, not only can the Japanese companies launch defect-free products, they can often do so with development times that are only a fraction of the western competitor's. For example, when Kodak first began to research the reasons why Fuji were making successful inroads into their cassette film market, they discovered among other things that whereas Kodak spent some two years on new product development, Fuji could do the same in only ten weeks! For Kodak, this represented a major competitive challenge. Eventually, the challenge was met, but only after a complete revision of all traditionally-held concepts of design organisation.

Just in Time (JIT or stockless production)

Unlike design, much has been written in the West about the phenomenon of stockless production in Japan. However, a great deal of the information is misleading. Many authors have intimated that JIT is achieved through computer-based scheduling programmes such as MRP II, etc. The fact is that stockless production is entirely related to the improvement process, which forms such an essential ingredient in Total Quality. It starts at the design stage and follows right though suppliers, production and to the ultimate customer. No one, anywhere in the supply chain, collects stocks. This makes a considerable difference to the balance sheet.

In the case of Matsuchita Refrigerators, half a day's stock is kept, and suppliers must supply *precisely* what is required every single working day (some higher levels of stock are allowed for suppliers who are some distance from the factory). Many westerners think that suppliers achieve frequent, small deliveries by holding stocks themselves. This is not true. If it were, then the cost would still be passed down one way or the other. The fact is that no stocks are held anywhere in the supply process. This is another example of a major Total Quality benefit which is not achievable simply through the application of ISO 9000-type systems. However, it is also true to say that JIT could not be achieved if systems and procedures were inadequate.

Employee involvement

As with most Japanese companies of any consequence, employee participation in the form of Quality Control Circles and employee suggestion schemes is very much in evidence. The plant currently has 120 such groups, 70 per cent of which are in the manufacturing functions. In this company 'safety circles' are also encouraged as a separate but equally important activity.

At Matsuchita Refrigerators, the circles are referred to as 'Reiki Jishu Kanri' ('RJK') activities, which translates roughly as 'voluntary control by refrigerators'. QC Circles are a fundamental aspect of Total Quality activities in Japan and are given a much higher profile than management project team activities. This is confusing to the westerner who understands the importance of project by project improvements as a means of improving overall organizational performance. In western companies, it can easily be shown that over

80 per cent of the cost of poor quality is management controllable, not worker controllable. Therefore, it would seem logical that the emphasis should be placed on management projects rather than QC Circle activities. Why should this be different in Japan? The answer is simple. Back in the 1950s, before the Japanese introduced Total Quality, management controllable problems were much the same as they are today in the West. From 1954 onwards, following Dr Juran's famous lectures, the Japanese began management-led project teams to tackle and solve such problems. However, many of the remedies resulted in managerial changes to organization which effectively eliminated the so-called management-solvable problems from the system once and for all. Consequently, the Japanese companies were eventually left with only the worker to operator controllable problems.

Let us consider the differences in the product design process referred to earlier in this case study. The following example is based upon the Matsuchita organization, but is similar in many respects to that found in other Japanese companies.

Design review system and assured quality approval system in the stage of new products development

Marketing team plan	
Merchandising concept approval	Obtain approval for product
	Design stage to reflect customer's quality requirements
Design specification Initial design review	Review of schedule, cost safety and productivity regarding the basic development concept

This will be followed by 'design drawing concept', followed by a preliminary design review of performance, reliability and target with design specifications, etc.

The objective at all stages is to achieve a smooth production system. The reviews are mainly conducted by the Engineering Department, but include other departments and specialists who will suggest improvements to the engineers. Successive stages include: trial sample drawing, trial run, test drawing review of quality assurance methods for testing parts, use of failure modes and effects analysis of all new mechanisms, detailed drawing review, drawing approval, trial mass production, manufacturing approval, mass production, delivery approval followed finally by test of market reaction.

All of this structure is written out in detail in flow diagram form and followed rigorously. Consequently, all of the really major management controllable problems which could emerge in the design process will be dealt with in a modern Japanese company as part of day-to-day management activities. What is left is the myriad of minor problems, few of which would enter the category of 'management controllable'. Consequently, these are dealt with either by QC Circles or through the suggestion scheme process.

At Matsuchita, QC Circles meet every first and third Wednesday in the month. These days are referred to as RJK days, and all circles are engaged in activities after 5 p.m. They also meet together. RJK activities at Matsuchita are highly developed and structured in the company's organization.

One novel feature is the *hearing tour*. This is a supportive activity in which managers, including the divisional manager, visit each circle during its meetings to hear what is being achieved and to give appropriate advice where necessary. According to Matsuchita, the purpose of this activity is to boost morale by ensuring a proper understanding of the processes and to give advice and instruction. All managers including the divisional manager, plant manager, managers and representative leaders, participate. The divisional manager and plant manager make a hearing tour every month.

Block judge meetings are conducted to evaluate progress and the results of circle activities when they submit 'concluding applications.' Block judging involves a block committee which meets on average once a month. The circle will present a report, lasting approximately 15 minutes, which is judged against specific criteria for which points are awarded. Prizes are given on the following basis:

Gold Prize	Over 85 points
Silver Prize	71–85 Points
Bronze Prize	Under 71 points

In addition to block judging there are 'Commendation and Presentations of Experiences'. The object of these is to give recognition and to provide a means of cross-fertilization between divisions of the organization. These meetings take place six times a year, and each section or division of the company will select one circle to make a presentation. The best example from each of these will be selected to make a presentation at an 'All Company Meeting'.

Prizes for these activities are as follows:

Gold Prize	2,000 yen/person
Silver Prize	1,000 yen/person
Bronze Prize	500 yen/person

(1,000 yen = approx. £4/$8)

As with most companies, commendation prizes are given further publicity by display in the workplace, and through in-house newspapers. Figure 3.3 shows how circle activities are usually evaluated on a plant-wide basis.

The format of QC Circles activities in RJK circles follows a universal approach:

1. The newly formed group will discuss QC activities in general before agreeing on a name, and the roles that its members will play.
2. The circle will select a theme.
3. Possible causes of problems are identified under the theme.
4. Troubleshooting activities are conducted to determine the true causes and to identify remedies.
5. The means of implementing the solution are decided.
6. Effectiveness of the solution is reviewed.

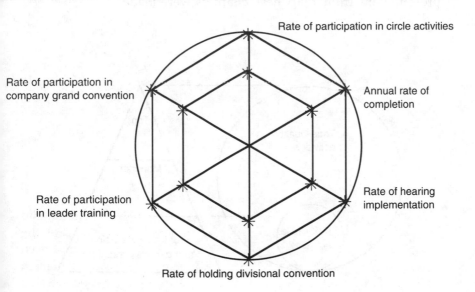

Figure 3.3   Circle activities evaluated on a plant-wide basis

Figure 3.4 indicates how RJK circles form part of Total Quality activities.

Matsuchita claim that:

1. The development of RJK activities are a part of Total Quality control activities.
2. RJK activities exist to:
    (a) contribute to continuous improvement and development of the corporation;
    (b) create a healthy workplace which respects people;
    (c) draw out infinite possibilities by creating people's potential.

These three concepts were originally identified by Professor Ishikawa and immortalized in the *Koryo to QC Circles*. Professor Ishikawa's contribution to the QC Circle movement has now been recognized in Japan through the creation of the Kaoru Ishikawa Award for QC Circles. The first award ceremony took place in Matsuyana City on 6 December 1990 at the 2590th QC Circle convention. During 1990 there were 183 QC Circle conventions throughout Japan in which a total of 142,408 delegates participated, and 3,941 reports of problem-solving were presented. On 5 November 1990 the All Japan QC Circle Convention took place at Hibiyu Public Hall, Tokyo: 2,276 people attended, and 18 presentations from 9 Japanese chapters were made.

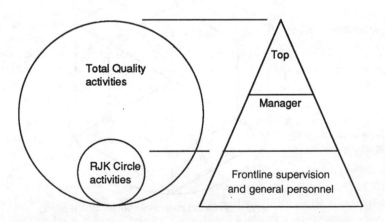

Figure 3.4   RJK circles as part of Total Quality activities

Suggestion schemes

One of the biggest contrasts between the attitudes of workers in Japan compared with the West can be seen in suggestion scheme results. In western organizations most suggestion schemes produce unimpressive results. Many are defunct or semi-derelict and only a small proportion of the workforce ever bothers to participate at all. In Japan it is different. In Toyota, for example, from a labour force of 40,000 people on average over 2,600,000 suggestions are made each year of which over 96 per cent are implemented. Unlike QC Circles the performance of suggestion schemes varies enormously from company to company both in the structure of the scheme and the results. In almost all cases, the suggestions are highly regarded but on the whole the financial awards are modest. At Matsuchita, the company actively encourages a large number of suggestions and targets about ten per month per employee. This is not unusual and is about the same as Fuji Electric Company, which manufactures vending machines. At Matsuchita about 50 per cent of the suggestions are adopted.

All suggestions are graded according to merit into eight categories, ranging from category 1 with an award of 20,000 yen down to category 8 with an award of 1,000 yen. Beyond this, there are further lower categories which do not make the grading scale but which merit an award of 200 yen. The top five categories are recommended up to the Matsuchita group level and collected from all divisions of the company.

Circle activities

A typical Quality Circle team presented a project related to the set-up and use of small tools. In this instance the team showed how they had reduced set-up time for their process from 8 minutes 4 seconds to 20 seconds with no further need for adjustment. On the same problem, the team had observed that the drill holder and brush had to be replaced for each size. They then asked: 'Could we use just one drill for all procedures?' The team subsequently ground a special drill which was stepped into two diameters. They called it the Yamanaka drill after the worker who thought of it. It eliminated the need for setting up altogether. Consequently, the original 8 minutes 4 seconds was now reduced to zero! This was estimated to save 715,500 yen per year.

A further development by another group demonstrated improvements in setting a positioning device whereby switching was reduced from 1 minute 25 seconds to 1 second, through the use of automatic adjustment on a conveyor using a pneumatic cylinder. Safety also improved as a result of fewer adjustments. Dispersion of component to component dimensional accuracy was reduced. Further savings resulted in:

1. The elimination of twelve tasks through foolproofing.
2. The revision of switching procedures and the creation of a standard operating manual.
3. The creation of a switching table for various activities.
4. Follow-up auditing with switching checksheet for each activity.

The circle said that their next step was to challenge other set-up times!

Basis for Total Quality at Matsuchita Refrigerator Company

Total Quality is obviously extremely well developed at Matsuchita. However, what is Total Quality, Japanese style?

In Japan, and increasingly elsewhere, Total Quality depends on the existence of policy management, but policy management means nothing if Total Quality is not being implemented. These two critical components of business organization and development are completely interrelated. In the words of Mr Tia Michiura, Managing Director of Amada Washing Company Ltd:

Certain individuals claim that it is impossible to introduce policy management at a time when TQC is not fully understood. By contrast, I was of the opinion that TQC could be learned through the imitation of policy management . . . TQC is designed to improve the corporate structure and its backbone is policy management. In TQC, emphasis is placed on making improvements to attain goals, by setting challenging goals, and by creating new methods of performance that are not merely a rehash of what has already been done . . . At Amada Washing we consider it inevitable at our current stage of TQC that profit plans and policy management be united. (*Societas Qualitatis*, Vol. 5, No. 1, Mar/April 1991)

Goal-setting is an integral feature of policy management and Total Quality Control. Projection of the key goal is often publicized by turning it into a slogan. In the case of Matsuchita Refrigerator Company the slogan is 'Quality First' (QF). Cascading down from this, each departmental manager is encouraged to develop a slogan in order to focus improvement activities towards key goals. At each lower level the slogan becomes more and more specific to the work of the section or area. The concept of policy management will be fully discussed in Chapter 9.

Summary

1. In all three examples (the Kanzanji Hotel, the Hawaiian Spa and Matsuchita Refrigerator Company) Total Quality formed the basis of the direction of the business.
2. In all three cases, participation in company projects designed to improve the overall competitiveness of the business (and in the case of the Hawaiian Spa the survival of the community), cascaded right through to the workforce in the form of QC Circles.
3. In all cases, Total Quality was driven by project by project improvement activities.
4. 'Market in/product out' was fundamental.
5. Both projects and QC Circle activities used decision-making based on facts.
6. In the case of Matsuchita, quality of supply was regarded as so important that virtually all components were made internally.
7. The company as a community is evident throughout.

4 Total Quality success stories 2

More TQ success stories! The case studies show:

- Management policy as the root of Total Quality
- 5S campaigns for tidy work
- Foolproofing to hold the gains
- Quality audits and review
- The potential of QC Circles

And concludes with Total Quality in practice in the United Kingdom

Kobayashi Kose

Lipstick, perfume and toilet water are usually associated with qualities of a different kind from those related to business processes. However, Kobayashi Kose Co. Ltd can honestly claim to contribute to both. Established in March 1946, Kobayashi Kose has a capital of ¥1,000,000,000, produces 1,782 products with a total nett weight of 12,000 tons and 94,000,000 products per year at the Sayama Plant near Tokyo and has 5,500 employees.

Its Japanese customers are at least as demanding as their western counterparts, and this requires continuous diversification of products and colours. In the case of lipstick there is a range of fifty colours, but they do not sell equally well, with the majority of sales obtained from just ten in the range, but the full range must be offered for consumer choice.

As in the case of the Matsuchita Refrigerator Company, Kose does not depend on robots. In fact, it is believed that robots would reduce plant efficiency. Consequently, production is highly labour-intensive. It is not surprising therefore that much of the focus on improvement activities relates to the involvement of the workforce. In a bid to achieve high quality at low cost, the company introduced Total Quality Control in 1977. This was decided after visiting a range of companies on an exchange visit basis – a very popular method of self-education in Japan. In 1980 the factory was awarded the Deming Award. This was a remarkable achievement, and it was in fact the first cosmetic factory to obtain the award. (Quality Control techniques, however, had been introduced around 1965.) As in the case of all other serious Total Quality developments, the programme at Kose was supported by policy management. This commenced with the president's policy simply stated as 'The spirit to pursue the true path'. From this a six-point major management policy was drawn up, aimed at developing qualified personnel and promoting their education. QC Circles, which form the backbone of Total Quality Control at Kose, developed from the next step which is 'Production Headquarters Policy'. This is stated as 'Create a positive atmosphere in the workshop by developing personnel and forming groups well disposed to learning and meeting challenges'.

Throughout Japan, QC Circles are highly regarded as one of the most important features of Total Quality Control, but at Kose, as elsewhere, Quality Assurance is more important. However, in order to bring about Quality Assurance and reduce costs, QC Circles are regarded as crucial.

Kose management also stress that QC Circles are not simply formed to bring about improvements. QC Circles are also a medium for effective education and training, and are particularly important to Quality Assurance. QC Circles at Kose do not compete with each other for prizes but, as with all other Japanese companies, awards are highly regarded both by the company and by the workers.

Again, as with other Japanese companies, a prime reason for the introduction of Quality Circles was to provide a means for the elimination of Taylorism. 'Taylorism' refers to the style of management originated by Fredrick W. Taylor in the United States, which effectively elevates all problem-solving upwards to increasingly higher levels of management. 'Management manages and people do' is a phrase often used to describe this style. Recognition of the serious drawbacks to this approach to management were first identified by the Japanese in the 1950s when they attempted to introduce American-style management. It was Professor Kaoru Ishikawa who first observed that the system was alien to Japanese culture and suggested that it would be worth experimenting with an alternative. His idea was to attempt to blend the best of Taylorism with the best of its crafts-based predecessor into a new model which would effectively eliminate the negative aspects of both. This plan led to the introduction of the QC Circles concept, which had its first recorded introduction at the Nippon Wireless and Telegraph

Company in 1962. By the end of that year over thirty-five companies had followed suit. Three years later, in 1965, Toyota began experimenting with QC Circles, but then shifted to zero defects in the late 1960s before returning to QC Circles in 1973. (The philosophy behind QC Circles will be examined in detail in Chapter 6.)

Taylorism had been applied at Kose Cosmetics. The company said that in those days, orders were given to the workers who were treated like robots. However, this was changed and workers were encouraged to put forward their own ideas. The effect was encouraging and education programmes were initiated. However, it soon became evident that education in the classroom on its own was not sufficient to motivate the workers. Education may make the worker aware, but it will not change anything. Unless the workers take the message to heart and really believe in what they have been taught, they will not be interested. Along with other Japanese companies autonomous and voluntary activities were found to be the answer, and these were developed enthusiastically at all levels of the company. However, not all circles have attained the levels of the best. About one-third of circles are regarded as excellent, one-third quite good and the rest are what are referred to in Japan as 'sleeping circles'. These are circles which, for one reason or another, have become inactive. This happens not only in Japan, but elsewhere. Many non-Japanese companies worry about this and think that it is an indication of waning interest. While, obviously, there is the possibility that something may be wrong, more usually it means that the group are just having a break. Given a favourable environment, the group will start up again when there is something interesting to deal with. Because of the voluntary nature of QC Circles, it is not possible to force teams to be active all of the time. The task for management is to discover how to motivate the sleeping circles. Kose must be quite good at this because their circles have won the Gold Prize at the All Japan QC Circle Convention five times since 1979. This is an outstanding achievement. One of their circles, the Kodama Circle, which is comprised entirely of part-time workers, won the Gold Prize in 1988. (Part-timers in Kose are similar to part-timers in the West and only work short shifts. In Kose bonuses are paid to all workers twice a year. The part-timers' bonuses are paid on a pro rata basis.)

Guided tours by the operators

The success of Japanese companies in the past thirty years has attracted considerable interest around the world. To give them credit, the Japanese have responded admirably and with considerable openness. Almost all of the best-known Japanese companies welcome foreign visitors and are willing to share a great deal of their experience. This is often embarrassing for the visitors who frequently observe that they do not think that they would have been as candid if the situation were reversed. Guided tours in leading Japanese companies occur so frequently that most companies devote an entire section of personnel to the task.

Kose Cosmetics, in common with some other companies, has adopted the novel approach of using process workers for this task. The objective is to further the workers' familiarization with the plant and all its activities, to develop a spirit of company-mindedness, and to increase the workers' awareness of the features of interest to the visitor. The workers obviously take pride in their appearance and, of course, the opportunity to do this work provides an attractive diversion from otherwise routine activities.

Taking a detour from the case example for a moment. A similar group of women at Komatsu formed a Quality Control Circle several years ago, and decided to produce a questionnaire for the visitors to elicit their impressions of the service provided and their impression of the plant. The questionnaire, which is a popular technique with Quality Control Circles, gave the circle a data base from which to select potential projects. The circle found that non-English-speaking visitors, who elected to choose the English-speaking tour guides did not always understand everything they were told, for while the Japanese tour guides spoke English reasonably well, it was not always comprehensible to the foreigner for whom English was a second language. The circle then collected data on the countries of origin of the visitors and the languages they spoke. They then asked the marketing department to identify the most important features which they felt the visitor should understand.

From all of these data, the circle used the 80/20 principle to identify the most common languages, and then had audio tapes produced which included a clear description of the items identified by the marketing department. This, together with other improvements, had a dramatic effect on the responses of foreign visitors. Following from this, the circle conducted a brainstorming session to think of ways of making the visitor more comfortable in a strange environment. One of the team members suggested that they buy small flags of all the foreign countries. The company cooperated with the circle. Then each day, before the visitors arrived, the circle would view the list of visitors and display the flags of the appropriate countries. Some companies do this anyway, particularly the Japanese, but the important thing in this case was the fact that the idea came from a Quality Control Circle.

The story of the Komatsu circle was told by the circle itself at the All Japan Quality Control Circle Convention in Tokyo in 1980.

This aside has been included at this point to illustrate the spirit of Quality Control Circles and it is obvious what effect the opportunity to be a tour guide would have on process workers who had hitherto been regarded as only an extension of their machines, desks or benches. In a typical western-style regime, no one would ask them anything or involve them at all.

Circles at Kose usually meet in the evening in the workers' own time but may meet more often when preparing a presentation. The main motivation is rivalry when one of the circles has won a Gold Prize. Circles are regarded as pleasurable pastimes, and the desire to beat another circle is strong, even though they are not encouraged to compete.

Six-point management policy

As in the case of Matsuchita Refrigerators, policy management is an essential part of Total Quality Control. Note the positioning. In the West many academics would have us believe that Total Quality Control is part of policy management. Under the structure of policy management, top management identify specific, high-level goals to be achieved. These are based on market research, competition and the internal needs of the business. From these high-level goals lower-level goals are distilled, which are deployed layer by layer down through the organization, becoming more and more parochial at each subsequent layer. All managers and workers are required to work within these goals and make suggestions as to how they may be achieved. The results of these achievements are recorded in management records. Within the structure, Quality Control Circles are not simply intended to make random improvements, but to implement the policy management point of view continuously, trying to achieve ever higher levels of performance, year after year.

The six policies of Kose Cosmetics are:

1. To produce high quality products.
2. To have an ideal sales system. Kose sell direct to retailers and therefore have an established rapport with them.
3. Correct public relations. Share knowledge with the customer and do not rely on expensive advertising campaigns. Always try to be honest with the customer.
4. Sound and steady management – the company will not increase borrowings unnecessarily, will manage prudently for the benefit of employees and the company as a whole, and, for the security of all employees, will expand gradually and carefully.
5. Development of personnel – humans are the most important company resource.
6. Labour–management relationships – try to achieve harmony and compromise between management and labour.

Supply policy

Kose believe it is very important to maintain high-quality products through correct relationships with their suppliers. Whenever an agreement is concluded with a new supplier, the standard of quality is established. Sometimes Kose will despatch their own quality experts to the supplier, who must pay for this service. However, Kose believe that it is to the benefit of the supplier in the long run. (Note the comments related to supplier policies in Chapter 2, and the Matsuchita case example in Chapter 3.)

History of Total Quality at Kose

1965 First application of Quality Control techniques and the introduction of zero defects and industrial engineering techniques.

1977 Total Quality Control introduced to production headquarters Period of education and training

1978 Period of Total Quality Control promotion

1979 Period of development

1980 Deming Prize awarded
The 'Weed Circle' awarded Gold Prize at the 'All Japan Quality Control Circle Conference'.

1981 Total Quality Control introduced into the whole company.

The 'PBX Circle' won the Gold Prize at the 'All Japan Quality Control Circle Conference'.

1982   The 'Kind Circle' won the Gold Prize at the 'All Japan Quality Control Circle Conference' making this three consecutive years. At the same time, the 'Foreman Circle' won the FQC Prize.

1983   The 'Sunflower Circle' won the NIKKEIQC Report Prize.

1984   The 'Ladybird Circle' won the Gold Prize at the 'All Japan Quality Control Circle Conference'.

1985   The 'Red Circle' won the Silver Prize at the 'All Japan Quality Control Circle Conference'. The 'First Circle' won the FQC Prize.

1986   The 'Daily Circle' won the silver prize at the 'All Japan Quality Control Circle Conference'. The 'Flower Circle' won the FQC prize.

1987   The 'Elegance Circle' won the FQC prize making this three consecutive years for Kose Cosmetics.

1988   The 'Echo Circle' won the Golden Prize at the 'All Japan Quality Control Circle Conference'.

On average, the 100 Kose circles complete 3.2 projects a year and make approximately 182 improvement suggestions per circle. The teams meet on average 3.8 times a month and spend approximately one hour per month per circle at meetings.

Komatsu

In the previous case study reference was made to one of the Quality Control Circles from Komatsu. Currently Quality Control Circles are a major part of Total Quality activities in the company.

Covering a massive 782,000m^2, Komatsu's Osaka plant manufactures large bulldozers and hydraulic excavators. The plant facility includes an integrated production system ranging from steel castings to finished products and a tractor technical centre for product research and development. The world's first radio-controlled bulldozers, the amphibious bulldozer and the world's largest-class bulldozers are all built at the plant. Total Quality activities began at Komatsu in 1960 following Japan's new trade liberalization laws which allowed foreign companies to enter into collaboration with Japanese companies. At that time Caterpillar, the American giant, formed a joint venture with Mitsubishi called Caterpillar Mitsubishi. Komatsu feared that the Caterpillar Mitsubishi initiative would drive them out of business and for a time their shares went below par.

The crisis forced Komatsu to analyze its weaknesses with the conclusion that quality was the principal problem, and a company-wide campaign was introduced in order to achieve drastic improvements in quality. With the assistance of JUSE the concept of Total Quality Control was studied in great depth in order to find ways of upgrading the equipment, then Total Quality was introduced. These intensive activities resulted in catching up with Caterpillar in both quality and in technology. Then they were able to export. The company's slogan was 'Encircle Caterpillar' and the programme *introduced from the top down from the Board of Directors right through to the workforce*. These days, the workers are regarded as being *the backbone of management*.

Between 1961 and 1963 a system was developed for policy management and new product development, and Quality Control Circles were introduced. At the same time, standardization was developed for working standards and engineering standards. In 1964 Komatsu won the Deming Award and in 1981 the much sought after 'Japan Quality Control Prize'.

Total Quality as related to the product is based on the spiral of progress in quality developed by Dr Juran, and blends with the Plan-Do-Check-Action cycle (see pp. 50–1). The spiral begins with market research to establish the conditions of use in the environment. The products are subjected to tough handling and rough environmental conditions. Therefore, it is important to make sure that the working conditions are fully appreciated at the design phase. This is followed by establishment of the quality targets, prototype testing and evaluation. These are the first Planning elements. The Do element commences with production and bought-out parts followed by inspection, shipment, before-sales service and sales. The Check element begins with after-sales service, followed by a second market research and then analysis of the results. This is to determine whether the original requirements have been met. Deficiencies identified at this the Action stage become improvement projects, followed by redesign, then production, and re-evaluation and hence the cycle is repeated continuously, in order to ensure continuous cycle by cycle improvement.

Policy management

This feature is very clearly articulated in the Total Quality plan at Komatsu. Policies are established from the dissemination of the president's annual policy, from which the plant managers' policy is developed and, subsequently, the policies and goals of line department. This also includes information from the long-range business plan and the long-range business plan for plant operations. These policies are also influenced by reports from departmental managers and the evaluation of plant activities and results from the previous year.

Policy or goal deployment, referred to in Komatsu as development of policies, develops into annual plans for each line activity divided into functions and separated into:

- Quality
- Cost
- Delivery categories
- Design

From this project team improvement activities and departmental manager's annual policies are developed, cascading down to annual plans for departmental activities, section activities, plans for staff and plans for Quality Control Circles (see Table 4.1).

Table 4.1. Summary of responsibilities at each level of management for the production of Total Quality Control activities.

Management	1.	Always at the forefront of TQC activities. Deploy policy.
	2.	Promotion of strategic TQC management.
	3.	Demonstration and diagnosis of the company policy.
Managers	1.	Deployment of the policy to the action plan.
	2.	'Leadership' within his own department/section.
	3.	Check and act, making improvement a daily activity.
Staff	1.	Self-enlightenment of QC sense and technology.
	2.	Assist and advise the line.
	3.	Attainment of manager's policy through technical assistance.
Supervisor	1.	On-the-job training for subordinates.
	2.	To provide work check for subordinates.
General worker	1.	Improvement of their own job using Quality Control Circle activities.
	2.	To maintain job standards.
	3.	5S activities to improve their work environment.

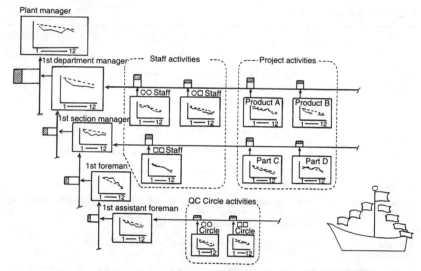

Figure 4.1 The Komatsu 'flag' chart (Source: Komatsu)

Policy control is effected by feedback at all levels on an hourly, daily, weekly, monthly, semi-annual or annual basis. The annual review effectively leads back to the president's goals and so the cycle begins again.

Wherever possible, goals are prepared in chart form (see Figure 4.1) and referred to as the 'flag' chart system, similar to the custom of fishing boats celebrating their catch by hoisting flags. The more flags the better the catch.

5S campaigns are extremely popular in Japanese manufacturing companies. Unfortunately, the 5S's do not translate into five words beginning with S in English. This is probably why previous authors have paid little attention to the concept. 5S campaigns are based on the belief that good products only come from a good environment. The 5S's are shown in Table 4.2.

Foolproofing

Throughout the Total Quality process, Komatsu make considerable efforts to raise awareness of the importance of closing problems once solutions have been found in order to prevent them recurring. Not only is the concept of foolproofing encouraged for improvement projects, it also highlights that foolproofing can be used to prevent

Table 4.2. The 5S's

	Definition	Aim
Seiri (remove waste)	Distinguish between needed and not needed items and throw away the latter	Preventive measure against waste
		Assurance of safety
Seiton (tidiness)	Keep things tidy so that they are available for use	Improvement of efficiency
		Assurance of safety
Seison (sweep)	To find minor defects while sweeping clean	Prevention of breakdown
Seiketsu (cleanliness)	Improvement of environment around the facilities to minimize deterioration	Maintenance and improvement of quality
Shitsuke (discipline)	Obey what has been decided	Standardization

problems *before* they occur. In the West, this happens where failure modes and effect analysis are used, but not usually on the line as a high-profile activity. Komatsu accept that carelessness is an unfortunate human characteristic and that mistakes will always occur. Therefore, by encouraging foolproofing in all activities, including jig and fixture design, such mistakes progressively become less and less likely.

Recognition of achievement is a fundamental of Japanese Total Quality Control and Komatsu are no exception when it comes to the promotion and encouragement of these activities. In Komatsu it is stated that the prize system is designed to achieve structural improvement in each company and to display the combined strength of the Komatsu group of companies by popularizing the QC concept throughout Komatsu-affiliated companies. The overall aim is to increase customer satisfaction, and prizes are also awarded to suppliers, affiliates, distributors and dealers.

Quality audit

These are conducted at all levels and the process works up through the organization to the annual president's audit. This is always a very thorough process and there is usually considerable preparation. In

Japanese companies, the president is normally one of the highest authorities on quality in the organization.

External Total Quality Control

More than half the costs at Komatsu are related to outside suppliers and other sources, therefore at Komatsu Total Quality Control extends through the supplying chain from vendor to distributor and dealers. Education, training and technical assistance are provided: there are Total Quality Control prizes. Typically, about seventy prizes are given each year.

Quality Control Circles

Quality Control Circle activities are enthusiastically encouraged at Komatsu, in common with most Japanese companies which practise Total Quality Control. Quality Control Circle activities are based upon the guidelines spelt out in the *Koreo to Quality Control Circles* published by the Quality Control Circle Headquarters of JUSE.

Komatsu describe the Quality Control Circle as:

- A small group formed voluntarily to perform QC activities within the workshop to which they belong.

This small group, with every member participating fully, carries on

- continuously, as part of company-wide quality control activities, self-development and mutual development, control and improvement within the workshop utilizing QC techniques.

The basic ideas motivating Komatsu Quality Control Circle activities are to:

1. Contribute to the improvement and development of the enterprise.
2. Respect other people and maintain a happy, bright workshop which offers meaningful work.
3. Show what people are capable of and eventually make sure they achieve their greatest potential.

Many people in the West think that Quality Control Circles are nothing more than small groups of workers trained to solve work-related problems. But this brief outline of Quality Control Circle activities at Komatsu indicates that the circles concept goes far deeper than this. In Japan, it is said that Total Quality Control cannot be performed without Quality Control Circle-type activities. Via the circles workers are involved in foolproofing, Total Productive Maintenance (TPM) activities and, of course, problem-solving and improvement suggestion activities. The Quality Control Circle provides a medium for communication, education and training, and encourages the understanding that each worker is a major contributor to the ongoing success of the organization. Through these activities workers are able to develop their abilities, pride and self-respect, and gain the respect of others.

Quality Control Circles are supported by a secure structure at Komatsu, which leaves no doubt about the company's degree of commitment.

Quality Control education is part of the ongoing development of QC Circles in Komatsu and other leading Japanese companies. Fortunately for the Japanese, the importance of this is well recognized by JUSE, which provides external support. Unfortunately, in the West the national equivalents to JUSE play no such role. Consequently, western QC Circles are starved of an important source of self-improvement. Western countries must address this problem if they are to close the gap with Japan.

Quality Control Circle support

Quality Control Circle promoter

One person from each section is selected to be the section's Quality Control Circle promoter. The promoters meet eight times a year for a Quality Control Circle Promoters Conference at which the yearly events of Quality Control Circles are discussed. Meetings are also held with promoters from other companies. These activities are supported by JUSE Quality Control Headquarters and the regional organization. Quality Control Circle promoters are similar to facilitators in western companies, but in the West, those persons are usually appointed by management and do not come from the section.

Quality Control Circle leaders

The leaders of Quality Control Circles meet once a month. The section managers may also attend these meetings. Topics discussed usually relate to other sections; information given about their activities; and there is an opportunity to discuss cross-departmental problems.

Total Quality in the United Kingdom

The case studies we have discussed have all been from Japan. But why not some British, European or even American cases? The remainder of this chapter will be devoted to this question. The reason why the Japanese companies were placed first is simple. Total Quality as a management concept was invented in Japan, and, until very recently, did not exist in the West or elsewhere in the Far East. Recently, western companies have experimented with almost all of the concepts, but *not* as a coordinated whole, and certainly not as an overall management philosophy. This is now changing and, with the advent of the Malcolm Baldrige Award, is changing rapidly in the United States. The European Foundation for Quality Management (EFQM) award, which is due to be launched in 1992, may change the state of affairs in Europe. However, the award will be restricted to EC member states and this should be made apparent in its title. Even today, with all of the work that is being done in major western companies to absorb Total Quality into their organizations, it is doubtful whether even the best match up to what the Japanese would agree could be called Total Quality-style management, particularly since there is no underpinning organization equivalent to JUSE. The examples included here, however, give accounts of companies that are well on the way, having recognized and accepted all the basic tenets of the concept, and that are already beginning to reap the rewards of this powerful management system.

Short Bros, Belfast

Short Bros manufacture aircraft and military products in the Belfast area of Northern Ireland, and employ around 8,800 people.

The essence of management thinking at Short Bros is best described by the managing director, Roy McNulty, in the first copy of Shorts' in-house publication *Changing Times* (March 1991).

At around the time that Shorts began to introduce Total Quality, the company was struggling with the problems of privatization and were looking for a buyer. There can be no doubt that this would tend to focus the mind, and it is interesting that in both this and in the Japanese examples initial moves to introduce Total Quality were sparked by a competitive challenge of some kind.

Eighteen months ago we boldly stated that, under the ownership of Bombardier, we were together 'en route to a new future'. Much has happened since then which is already shaping this future. The Company has been reorganised and recently this has been fine-tuned. We have launched several new projects with enormous potential and expanded others to unprecedented levels of production. Visitors to the Company are amazed at the physical changes – the progressive modernisation of our facilities is certainly in harmony with a Company that is moving forward.

One initiative that started a couple of years before privatisation was Total Quality. As the initial debate progressed, it became clear that while Total Quality introduces some new tools and techniques, *it is fundamentally a concept that is about realising the potential of our people*. Last November, at the Company Prizegiving, Raymond Royer, President and Chief Operating Officer of Bombardier, stated that the only thing that differentiates Shorts as a Company from our global competitors is our people. The quality, and therefore the effectiveness, of any Company is a direct reflection of the quality and effectiveness of its people. Total Quality can be viewed as a way of releasing the untapped potential of our total workforce, a tool which will give us the competitive advantage to make us world leaders.

We demonstrated our belief in the importance of Total Quality for achieving profitability (and therefore a secure future for us all) by making it an Executive Agenda item for 1990/91. That is to say the Management Committee singled out Total Quality as one of the three areas that demanded top priority as we strive to improve our business performance. It should be clearly understood by *everyone* that Total Quality is fundamental to the turnaround of Shorts. We *must not* make the mistake of some British industries (e.g. the motorcycle industry) of believing that our current performance and levels of improvement are good enough. We face new demands and expectations in today's competitive market place. If we are to keep ahead of emerging competition from countries like Korea, Brazil, Japan, etc., we must strive to *continuously improve everything* we do.

We should be in no doubt if we do not continuously improve and achieve ever higher levels of performance *someone else will*. If we cannot meet our customers' ever rising expectations *someone else will*. If we cannot bid for work at a competitive price *someone else will*.

When he visited Shorts, Dr Deming, the well-known quality 'guru', was quizzed on whether he saw Total Quality as an important option and he responded. 'You do not have to do this, *survival is not compulsory!*'

Since the Total Quality Programme was launched, over 8000 employees have attended at least one half-day awareness session. The overriding message from those who developed this training was that *the vast majority of people in Shorts are keen to contribute to the turnaround*. This puts a considerable responsibility on Management to allow and encourage people to use their skills and experience to improve every aspect of our business.

Many employees have already demonstrated what can be done as they have tackled problems through the Total Quality programme and achieved levels of performance previously not thought possible.

This newsletter is an example of continuous improvement of the Total Quality Programme. At a series of Management Seminars in August 1990, the general message emerging was that of a lack of communication of Total Quality in Shorts. It is our intention to use the pages of this newsletter to keep you updated on Shorts and our journey towards becoming the industry leader in each sector of our business through Quality, productivity, innovation and satisfied customers.

'Quality is never an accident,' John Ruskin said, 'it is always the result of intelligent effort.' We must make planning for Quality an integral part of the way we do business.

ROY McNULTY
Managing Director
(from 'Firmly en route through Total Quality', *Changing Times* 1, March 1991)

The Total Quality programme was launched in 1987 and, to date, is probably one of, if not *the* best in the United Kingdom. The reason for their success is their obvious commitment and resolve to succeed. Total Quality at Shorts was initiated by the board of directors, who had decided to practise what they were about to preach, by forming themselves into a Quality Council to steer the overall programme. Quality Circles were then formed in the Aircraft Division and in the Military Products Division, each led by one member of the higher level council (Figure 4.2). The object of this was to 'back link' each of the two lower-level councils to the Board Council, the latter thereby providing an umbrella and vehicle for cross-fertilization in the programme as it cascaded down through the organization.

At each major function, such as R & D, Operations, etc., further Quality Councils were formed. The object of this was to ensure a sense of local ownership, while at the same time ensuring that

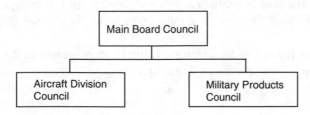

Figure 4.2   Backlinking to the Main Board Council

the problem selection process was as parochial as possible. These councils also 'back linked' upwards.

Training

Training at Shorts is provided through a 'Total Quality Centre' which, it is claimed, has embarked on the largest schedule of training ever known at Shorts, educating all company employees in the basics of Total Quality. New employees are also made aware of Total Quality at induction with follow-up sessions after six months.

The company-wide Total Quality programme has the objective of reducing the cost of poor quality on a project by project basis by £45 million. In 1990/1 some 220 projects saved £6 million and in 1991/2 they were on track towards saving over £7.5 million through 300+ projects. Over 350 project team leaders have been trained in all the techniques of quality improvement. The initial efforts of Shorts also won the coveted National Training Awards in 1989.

The staffing of the Total Quality Centre in Shorts is novel. Managers are taken off the line to work in the centre on a full-time basis for approximately 18 months. Then they return to line duties. Having run the centre and conducted the training for that period, it is believed that managers will become totally committed to the concept. Ultimately, all managers will have this experience.

The role of the centre is to:

- Coordinate all Total Quality activities throughout the company and interact at all levels with the Total Quality structure.
- Support the Quality Council in developing the Total Quality strategy.
- Support the Divisional Councils and Functional Quality Teams.
- Ensure that the project by project approach is effective (including maintenance of computerized records of all Total Quality projects).
- Develop Total Quality with the company's supplier base.
- Expand the use of Statistical Process Control in the company.
- Develop Total Quality in conjunction with the Ulster Business School.
- Organize Team Leader Training Courses in response to demand.
- Publicize achievements in Total Quality.

Role of the company Quality Council

- To determine how Total Quality can best be used to enhance business performance.
- To provide visible leadership in the drive to make Total Quality a way of life.
- To review Total Quality company-wide and ensure activities are effective.
- To agree overall policy and education for Total Quality.

Role of the divisional Quality Council

- To lead and control Total Quality activities within each division.
- To define and publicize Total Quality policies and objectives.
- To determine priorities for Total Quality projects.
- To allocate human and financial resources to nominated projects.
- To set the measurement criteria for project evaluation.
- To provide overall support and encouragement for Total Quality activities.

Role of the functional Quality teams

- To lead and control Total Quality activities within each area.
- To provide support and guidance for Total Quality activities.
- To publicize Total Quality activities in their own areas.
- To ensure the project team leader is fully briefed and trained.
- To monitor project progress.
- To ensure that project commencement and completion forms are filled in and returned to the Total Quality Centre.
- To implement fully the remedies and ensure that the gains are held.

Amersham International

This is an extract from an article by Amersham International Quality Improvement Manager.

'The challenge for us in the life sciences business of Amersham International was to successfully blend Quality Circles into our Quality Improvement programme. The first problem was deciding when to start them, but this became clear from the people themselves. A year into our programme there was an enthusiastic demand for involvement, with people from all areas volunteering to take part. So we decided to start Quality Circles, but first on a trial basis – thinking big but starting small – then, step by step, more people joined in as we learned more and more about what worked best in our business. But we were careful not to compromise on the best principles of the problem-solving process. Our first circle was in one of our production areas and involved everyone in the work area. This glassware is made up of the flasks, beakers, etc., which are essential for the chemical synthesis that form the basis of their work. They found that the problem was not carried by lack of glassware but by poor organization in their laboratory. They introduced a new system which was an immediate success. The result was zero stock-outs in the next nine months!

The second trial circle was in a different production area. This group investigated the availability of some of the smaller, but vitally important pieces of equipment used in their work. Their analysis, of course, eventually showed that breakage of equipment – rather than lack of it – was at the root of the problem. If they could stop the breakages they would boost the availability as well as save £12,000 per year in maintenance costs. So they designed a simple clip and holder to prevent their fragile instruments from being accidentally knocked over and broken.

Our Product Development Group also contributed to our trials. They found over 30 per cent of their dispensing pipettes were inaccurate. This was an unexpected result and cast doubt on the validity of some of their results. It prompted them to liaise with their supplier and come up with a routine for regular calibration of all their pipettes. They also designed a record chart which is publicly displayed to ensure the routine is followed and that the gains are held. These successes have made it easier for us to gradually expand Quality Circles to most areas and laboratories in life sciences. The are proving to be a great success and are popular with those taking part. (Alan Hodgson, Quality Improvement Manager, Amersham International)

H.J. Heinz, UK

Figures indicated that the cost of failure at H.J. Heinz was £49 million per annum.

'We have to compare ourselves to the best,' said Roger Alcott, 'and in so doing we set out a table of crucial factors; brand share, volume, innovation and Quality. No longer could we rely on customer complaints to gauge failure.

'And it must be remembered that at the start of the last decade, our competitors were own-label products from the retailers who were also our customer, which is why we had to find a sustainable alternative to our existing initiative – HII – Habitual Incremental Improvement. We had the will, but lacked structure, training and understanding.' (Roger Alcott, Planning and Training Manager, H.J. Heinz, UK)

Perhaps, though, the most memorable thing that Alcott said was that Heinz is learning to recognize and respond positively to reward success, not only punish failure. Such changes are difficult in mature company cultures, but Heinz has begun the long march.

Summary of Chapters 3 and 4

The case examples were selected because each one brought out a variety of points which form the essence of Total Quality. They were selected from a range of industries to indicate that Total Quality has no basis in any particular *niches* but is universal. Total Quality represents a unique approach to the direction and management of an organization.

Specific points

1. In every case, Total Quality was introduced by the directors of the organization in response to a perceived competitive threat. In the case of the Kanzanji Hotel, the threat came from a powerful hotel chain. Total Quality was introduced into the Hawaiian Spa simultaneously with its conversion from being a coal mine. Matsuchita introduced Total Quality as part of an overall programme, but also because competition in the Japanese white goods market is fierce. Kose Cosmetics introduced Total Quality because of keen competition, as did Heinz in its battle with own-label brands. Total Quality was initially introduced into Shorts by its Managing Director as part of its strategy to come to terms with privatization and the loss of government protection. Komatsu introduced Total Quality as a means of countering the threats from the Caterpillar Matsuchita joint venture. In the end, the improvements at Komatsu almost put Caterpillar out of business.

2. In each case, the initiative was started and led by the president and Board of Directors. Subsequently, these groups have regarded Total Quality as the only way to run their businesses. Commitment is total and in the case of most of the Japanese examples, has spanned several decades in most cases. Others, such as Toyota, Nissan, Nippon Steel and the main Matsuchita organization, can trace their first commitment to Total Quality-style business development back to the late 1940s. In the western examples, experience in Total Quality is too recent to judge such long-term development, but the commitment is strong at the top, and the impact on organizational improvement so impressive, and the culture change so marked, that it is hard to see how the resolve could dissipate for any other reason than for major changes in company leadership.

3. In all cases, the process begins at the top with policy management, followed by goal-setting and deployment down through the organization to the workforce.

Intensive use of project by project improvement teams at managerial level followed by the extensive development and support of Quality Control Circle teams and suggestion schemes are the backbone of the process. Policies lead to goals; goals lead to projects and improvement ideas. It is too early for the suggestion schemes in Japanese companies to be equalled in the West, but in companies like Shorts, Amersham and Heinz, this is only a matter of time. At Toyota, from a labour force of 40,000 people, there are over 2,600,000 improvement suggestions a year, of which over 96 per cent are implemented. At Matsuchita Refrigerator factory, one employee made ten suggestions a day, on average! This is also achievable in the West once the concept of continuous incremental improvement has become established, but more work on culture change will have to take place before this can be achieved.

4. The Matsuchita examples show what can happen in a manufacturing environment in new product development. Only a fraction of the deficiencies normally present in the first production units normally experienced in western companies were present. This is typical of Total Quality companies in Japan and explains why the Japanese are so effective with the launch of new products. Gone are the days when the next inspector is the customer, who finds the problem which results in premature product upgrades and expensive product recalls. These problems, even today, tend to cripple many of their western competitors. Another feature of Japanese product development is the short product-development cycles. Kodak is a prime example (see p. 55).

5. Quality Control Circles form a significant part of Total Quality in Japan, but this is not the case in western companies. There is a good reason for this. In Japan, the management aspects of Total Quality began 10–12 years before Quality Circles were conceived by Professor Ishikawa. Dr J. M. Juran introduced project by project improvement to the Japanese in 1954 as a management activity, not as a concept for the workers. When the costs of poor quality are identified, and priorities determined using the Pareto (80/20) principle, the result

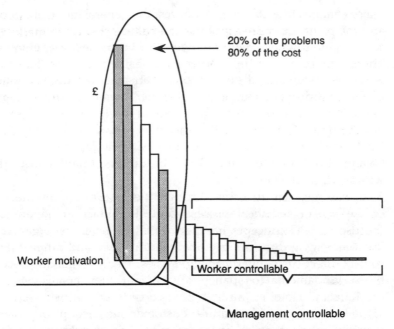

£

20% of the problems
80% of the cost

Worker motivation

Worker controllable

Management controllable

Figure 4.3 Relative cost of management and worker controllable costs

can be depicted diagrammatically (Figure 4.3). The figure shows that while 80 per cent of the problems are controllable by the workers, this will only affect 20 per cent of the costs. Whereas, while 20 per cent of the problems can be controlled by management these account for 80 per cent of the costs. Dr Juran's advice to the Japanese was that they should focus on the management controllable problems first. This they did with impressive effect. After 1954, as each problem area was addressed, the problem-solving process moved layer by layer down through the hierarchy. Eventually, soon after 1960, when most of the major management controllable problems had been dealt with, it was time to address the remainder. However, there is another reason for addressing the worker controllable problems other than to cut the costs and to improve quality. One management controllable problem yet to be tackled was motivating the workforce. The concept of worker involvement in problem-solving was seen to be attractive as a motivational concept, and therefore management's responsibility was not simply a means for a problem-solving exercise.

The solution of management controllable problems resulted in major changes to systems, procedures, the general mode of operation and the planning of new products and processes. Consequently, the source of new management problems had been effectively eliminated. There only remained the worker controllable problems. Since these would be diverse, and new problems arising from the introduction of new products, technology, customer demands and ever-rising expectations of consumers, there would never be an end to these opportunities. Consequently, as the years passed, the Quality Control Circle concept became the main activity in Japanese-style Total Quality Control. From this Total Productive Maintenance (TPM) was a natural development.

6. It was not easy to show through the case examples the extent of the use of statistical process control. In fact, in Japan today, the use of SPC concepts has permeated all levels of organization. Even managing directors use Shewhart average and range charts to control direct costs, overheads and sales. Decision-making based on facts is fundamental to Japanese-style management at all levels. Recall the Kanzanji Hotel example, where considerable efforts were made to make the intangible feature 'customer satisfaction' or 'customer reaction' into a tangible measure, albeit using subjective data via the video camera, as well as the use of questionnaires, which are extensively used throughout Japanese industry. The author has made a habit of filling in the questionnaire in the in-flight magazine on Japan Airlines, and has, without fail, always received a detailed personal reply to comments made.

Conclusion

It can be seen from these examples that Total Quality is not something to be introduced lightly. We are looking at an extremely complex and multifaceted concept, which, as it is developed and cascaded down through an organization, will effectively begin to reduce costs, improve professionalism beyond measure, and create a totally new culture and work ethic. This cannot be achieved by chance, nor can it be delegated. It is a tough assignment for the chief executive because he or she alone must lead the way. Many will not be prepared for this, for it is a major commitment. But such people do have a choice: they can carry on as before and hope to survive, or make way for others who do have the commitment. One thing is certain. Total Quality has developed beyond the point where its relevance is open to question.

Currently, Europe is lagging behind the United States, where companies are now embracing the idea of Total Quality with enthusiasm. Inertia and cynicism abound in Europe, and its obsession with ISO 9000 and third party assessment is costing it dear with its drain on resources and deflection of attention from the real issues. This obsession has probably cost British industry alone ten years of Total Quality development time.

The following chapters deal with each of the main concepts of Total Quality, beginning with statistical process control and working through the relevance of ISO 9000, Quality Control Circles, weaving in JIT, TPM and suggestion schemes where they are appropriate. Finally, the questions of how, when and where to get started will be discussed in Chapter 9.

5 Statistical process control

A market is never saturated with a good product but it is very quickly saturated with a bad one.

Henry Ford

This chapter examines how statistical analysis can be harnessed to the power of Total Quality for full employee involvement. And covers:

- The power and uses of statistical process control
- Variable and attribute data in diagnosis of problems
- Total Productive Maintenance activities
- Frequency and concentration diagrams for simple data analysis

Many readers may be tempted to skip this chapter, but please don't! The order of the chapters in the book is deliberate. Statistical process control is placed in the middle because it is fundamental to the core of Total Quality activities. The object of this chapter is not to teach statistics but to demonstrate its importance to Total Quality. Most directors and managers in western companies shy away from statistics, thinking that they may not be relevant to them or that they apply only to small specialist groups in their organizations. This is unfortunate and an indictment of generations of lecturers and authors of mathematical works. The resulting cost or loss to society as a result of this deficiency cannot easily be quantified in financial terms, but must be extensive. What is more, the most important practical and usable techniques are for the most part blindingly simple and do not require a grasp of advanced mathematics to obtain their benefits.

All too often, authors are so mesmerized by their mastery of the subject that they overlook the fact that their purpose is to teach something that is actually useful. This does not require the most sophisticated theories, but generally the most basic. Sometimes the application of the simplest concepts can and does produce stunning results. This chapter is devoted to the proof of this observation by case study.

It was stated in the previous chapter that Japanese companies operating Total Quality-style management attempt to manage everything through decision-making based on facts rather than theoretical arguments. Before turning to the case examples, for the benefit of those readers who are somewhat hesitant about the applicability of statistically-based techniques, we shall introduce a few fundamentals and show the basic simplicity of statistical concepts.

For all practical purposes – and this chapter is intended to be purely practical – there are basically only two kinds of data:

- Variable data
- Attribute or countable data

Variable data means exactly what it says it is. It embraces everything that varies in discrete, incremental steps, such as that described on a digital or analogue scale. Data include such characteristics as dimension, weight, speed, time, voltage, current, capacitance, viscosity, moisture content, etc.

Attribute data include all right/wrong, good/bad, is/isn't, did/didn't, error/no error, missing/not missing, etc., situations.

There is a sub-group to this type of data called subjective data, because it is subjective to the senses, and includes activities such as wine or tea tasting, loudness when measured by the ear instead of an instrument, feel, smell, etc.

At this point, many western textbooks would take the reader into probability theory, binomial, Poisson and normal distributions, before attempting to give the reader simple practical tools. Sometimes they never do. In Japan it is different. Long before taking the student on excursions into mathematics, they provide the student with simple and practical tools, which work and produce results. The Japanese have also found that over 80 per cent of the problems which can be solved in industry require nothing more than the simplest of knowledge. Of the two types of data, probably 80 per cent of all applications relate to attribute rather than variable data. All attribute data behave in much the same way, with some reservations.

Attribute data always begin from zero possible occurrences and then proceed through 1, 2, 3 . . . onwards. For example, a roll of cloth may have zero, one, two, three or more oil stains, marks or tears. In theory it could have an infinite number. A consignment of tin cans could contain zero, one, two, three or more damaged or dented items up to and including the total population.

If the organization has never attempted to use statistically-based methods to collect or analyze data, or is primarily concerned with the use of simple data collection and analysis techniques for problem-solving or for use by operators or other direct labour, there is no need to distinguish between the two examples. In reality there is an important difference between data that can theoretically go to infinity, and data, as in the case of the cans, that are finite, e.g. all cans dented. This difference becomes an issue when contractually binding sampling plans are to be used, but not, as mentioned, in problem-solving. If attribute data are plotted in chart form, they will always produce predictable patterns, which will vary depending on the average number of occurrences of the feature being observed. Suppose a sample of fifty cans were taken at random from production, and the number found to be defective recorded in chart form. If the average number of defects in the sample was 10 per cent the result of a series of samples could be shown diagrammatically (see Figure 5.1). A chart like this could be produced by almost anyone.

Now suppose an improvement had been made to the process, and data again plotted to see the effect. The results are shown in Figure 5.2.

Figure 5.2 shows that the new process is better. Note that, in both cases, the actual number of defects found in the sample varies,

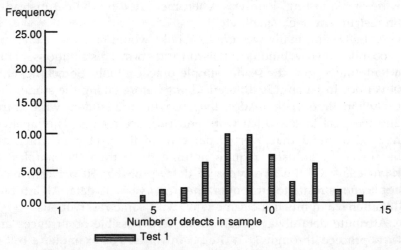

Figure 5.1 Frequency diagram to show number of defects in a sample

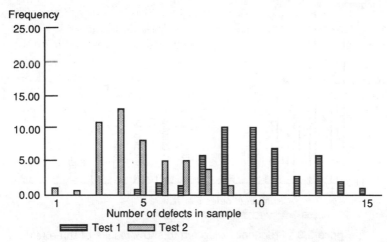

Figure 5.2   Frequency diagram to show comparison between tests before and after improvements to process

and this will always be the case, even though the process may be stable throughout the sample period. This is due to random or chance variations in the process and in the choice of sample items. However, the pattern for a given coverage number never changes, and the actual results will be almost but not quite identical to those that would be predicted mathematically.

Now let us take the situation one stage further, and suppose that further improvements had been made. The result might well look like Figure 5.3.

Again, there can be no question that improvements have been achieved. This is a hypothetical example to demonstrate the simplicity of using frequency diagrams for attribute data.

Now let us consider two actual examples of this method.

Case 1 The leaky catheter bag

Having to wear a catheter bag is unfortunate. Wearing a leaky catheter bag is worse, so it is hardly surprising that the company which makes this product, conducts leak tests on 100 per cent of its products. The test requires that the product be emersed in a tank of water to a depth of approximately $5\frac{1}{2}$ inches. Air is then pumped into the bag at a pressure of 6 p.s.i.. Bubbles indicate any leaks.

A project team concerned with the problem of leaks collected a

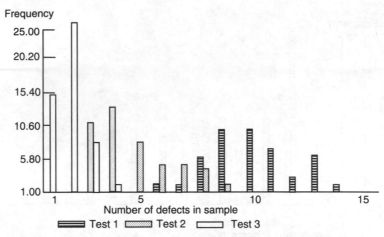

Figure 5.3   Frequency diagram to show results of three tests

large sample of batch cards and then plotted the number of leaky bags per shift. The results are shown in Figure 5.4.

The results do not look like the curves shown in Figures 5.1–3 and the team had difficulty in finding a reason why. One of the team members suggested the possibility that the chart might be concealing three separate sets of data. The question then arose, what might cause the difference? One member remarked that there were three different welding heads: one in the store, one on the machine and the third being cleaned. Perhaps there was a head to head difference. When the data were replotted on this basis, this was found to be the case (see Figure 5.5).

The team then had to find out why one of the heads was better than the other two. When they found the answer, they were able to bring the other two up to the level of the best. The total time spent on the data collection and analysis was only a total of three hours. The cost of the improvements negligible. But the benefit saved the company thousands of pounds per annum in defect costs, not to mention the improved reputation with its customer, the Department of Health & Social Security. The technique was blindingly simple and was used by a team of process workers!

Case 2 Bandage knitting needles

In the same company as the catheter bag example, another group was concerned with downtime on tubular bandage knitting machines.

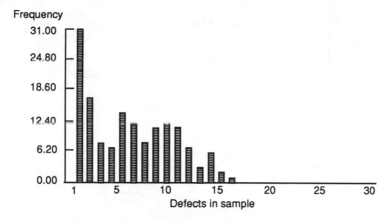

Figure 5.4 Frequency diagram to show number of leaky catheter bags per shift

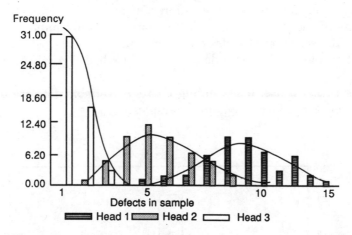

Figure 5.5 Frequency diagram to show number of leaky catheter bags according to welding head

The team discovered that a principal cause of downtime was broken latches on the needles (see Figure 5.6).

Using the same technique as in the previous example, the team discovered a supplier to supplier difference, which was hitherto unknown. The remedy was simple and made an immediate impact on productivity and cost.

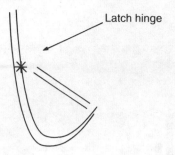

Figure 5.6   Defect in latch hinge

Variable data

Theoretically, the treatment of variable data is quite different from attribute data. This is true when more sophisticated techniques are used, but again, for practical purposes, in project work and for very simple control purposes, the differences are really quite small. The means of plotting the data are identical, the only minor difficulty being the selection of scales on the graph.

When plotted, variable data usually look like Figure 5.7, but not always.

For practical use, the resulting charts of variable data are usually very revealing. Here are a few examples.

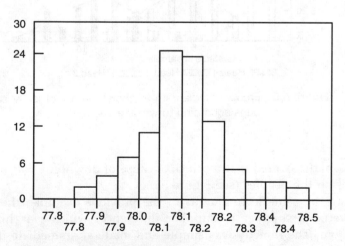

Figure 5.7   Variable data chart

Service time – counter staff

When the average service time spent dealing with customers in a bank, shop, check-in at a hotel or other similar data is plotted, the collective result for a number of staff looks like Figure 5.8.

The information that comes from this is useful and can determine the number of staff required to meet a given level of demand. It also indicates the dispersion of fast and slow transactions. This dispersion may be due to differences in customer demands. If it is possible to separate the data by type of transaction, the results look like Figure 5.9.

It is obvious from the data that time to cash cheques is markedly shorter than for currency conversion and for general enquiries. By making separate booths for each of these, queuing time for cashing cheques can be considerably reduced. Of course, most banks do this, but the data clearly indicate why.

In the above example, the data were organized by task, and it can be noted that there is a wide dispersion around the average time for general enquiries. This might be expected because the nature of each enquiry will be different. However, if the data are separated out so that individual counter assistants are recorded separately the result may be as in Figure 5.10.

In this case, it can be seen that Assistant A is quicker than Assistants B and C. Furthermore, not only does Assistant C take longer on average, but the curve is not symmetrical. C is obviously having difficulty with some tasks which presumably present no problems

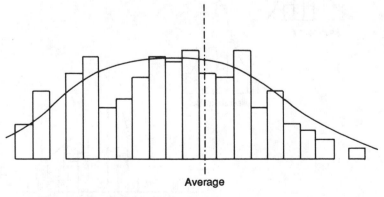

Average

Figure 5.8   Variable data chart to show average service time for a number of staff

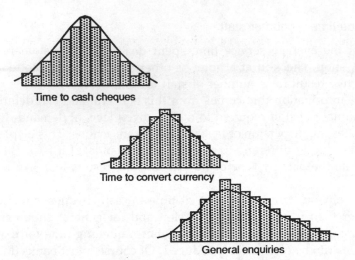

Time to cash cheques

Time to convert currency

General enquiries

Figure 5.9   Variable data chart to show service time by type of transaction

for A and B. This can be analyzed further, and a remedy perhaps found by giving Assistant C training. The reasons for A's improved overall performance could also be studied further, and again it may be possible to discover the differences in technique to bring B and C up to A's level. It may also be possible through QC Circle activities to give A, B and C the opportunity to discover this for themselves.

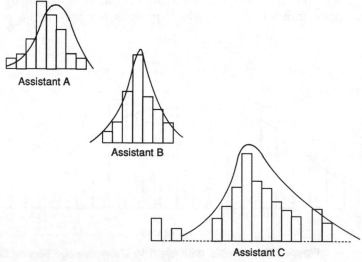

Assistant A

Assistant B

Assistant C

Figure 5.10   Variable data chart to show service time by assistant

It can be seen from the foregoing example that much can be revealed from the simplest techniques, techniques that can be used by anyone, without any need for mathematics or statistical theory. Again the question arises. If this is fine, why are these methods rarely used in industry? The answer is also simple. People are frightened off by the language of the statistician before they ever discover this. In Japan they have no such inhibitions. Techniques such as those described above are taught in simple language, often using *Beano* and *Dandy*-style educational programmes to empower the workers. Through training in these basic skills, Japanese workers have managed to solve millions of problems at the level described in this test. Before moving on, let us take a look at some further examples of the power of these simple techniques.

Case 2 revisited – measuring the finished product

The examples of the catheter bags and latches for knitting bandages were both real examples obtained from the first day of a three-day course in basic data collection and analysis for line managers and supervisors. None had any previous educational background, yet in a short time, thousands of pounds had been saved.

On the second day, the participants were introduced to data collection using variable data. One group decided to check the length of bandage in the finished goods stores. Printed on the boxes, the length was specified as being 10 metres. About fifty boxes were selected at random and lengths measured. The results are given in Figure 5.11, and show that, on average, the company was giving away over 1 metre of bandage. It was estimated that this had probably been going on for some thirty years, and cost the company £35,000 per year for each separate size of bandage. For a small company, this was a great deal of money. The worst aspect was the fact that the customer was probably totally unaware of the gift. How many people measure bandages? (Certainly none would make a supplier to supplier comparison.)

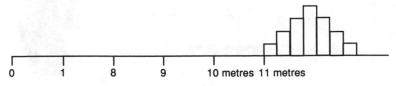

0	1	8	9	10 metres	11 metres

Figure 5.11   Diagram to show average length of bandage

The reason for the variation lay in the process. Years ago when the process was first developed, it was found that measuring length on a high-speed/high-volume process was not easy. An engineer had observed that it would be easier to measure weight than length. He also postulated that there would be a fairly close correlation between the two. Consequently, he developed the apparatus below (Figure 5.12).

The operator attached the end of a new piece of bandage to a rotating spindle protruding from the side of a set of weighing scales. The rotation of the spindle wound the bandage onto the spindle which was connected mechanically to the weighing apparatus. Thus, as the bandage wound on, its scale reached a certain level. It was concluded that the length of bandage was approximately 10 metres. It was an ingenious device, but unfortunately not properly thought out. Presumably, when the apparatus was first set up some trials were conducted to establish the relationship between weight and length. However, clearly, this was subsequently never checked. In fact, there are too many variables for this technique to work with any degree of accuracy. These variations include:

- Tension in the yarn.
- Pitch of warp and weft.
- Moisture content.
- Weight of yarn.
- Stretch on the machine used to weigh.
- Operator to operator differences.

Fortunately, an engineer found that it was possible to measure length just as easily as weight by attaching a small wheel under the

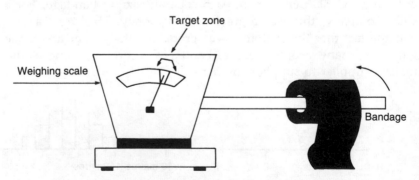

Figure 5.12   Scale to measure weight of bandage

yarn as it was spun onto the spindle, and to dispense with the scales. The savings that ensued from these three simple exercises resulted in a Board meeting, following which statistical techniques were introduced throughout the plant at all levels. Frequency diagrams appeared everywhere!

Case 3 Plant maintenance

Using the same technique as described above, an engineering company obtained the cooperation of its workers to collect data on plant breakdowns. This involved the use of both simple attribute and variable data.

The attribute data were used on a sampling basis to identify whether or not plant was running, and then used from time to time to detect whether any changes had occurred resulting from improvements made. This is the type of project which would be carried out by a QC Circle on TPM (Total Productive Maintenance) activities in Japan (Figure 5.13).

Variable data were plotted for time to failure on certain components which were known to have a relatively short life. Figure 5.14 shows time to failure for feed fingers on semi-automatic machine tools.

If failures occur during the shift, the disruption is high and cost around two hours of downtime for each occurrence. That may not seem a great deal, from every 260 hours of operation, but in fact the real cost is much higher, not in lost time, but in the accumulation

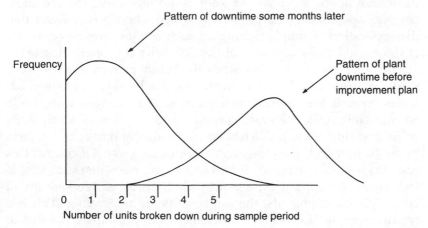

Figure 5.13 Attribute data to show number of plant breakdowns

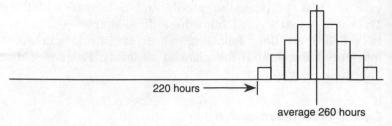

220 hours ⟶|

average 260 hours

Figure 5.14 Time to failure for feed fingers on semi-automatic machine tools

of work in progress (most of which is not progressing) and reduced predictability of production output which in turn leads to stock-outs, and to the keeping of exclusive stocks in finished goods warehouses to safeguard against this. These costs appear on the balance sheet as stocks and inventory and also suffer depreciation and incur interest charges. Worse, these unscheduled breakdowns result in lower levels of plant utilization. The usual counter to this would be to obtain additional plant, and of course appropriate manning levels. These will appear as direct costs on the profit and loss account, fixed but depreciating assets on the balance sheet, and will tie up precious working capital, and also demand additional supportive maintenance activities.

Typical plant utilization in western companies can be as low as 30 per cent availability and rarely higher than 70–80 per cent, so these costs are significant. By contrast, in Japanese companies, plant utilization of 92–96 per cent is normal even for the most complex operations. The position is worse when it is realized that the application of simple techniques such as those described in this chapter could make up much of the difference if properly applied.

Returning to the examples, when the failure pattern was revealed, it was agreed that the feed fingers should be replaced every 200 hours, even if they were still functional. The changes were made outside shift time, therefore causing no disruption of work flow, while ensuring better predictability of scheduling times, no log jams in production and, therefore, less work in progress. Of course, this one idea will not change the world on its own, but when such simple techniques are applied on a plant-wide basis by all workers on all critical plant components, the full benefits are astounding. This is a typical example of continuous incremental improvement applied to a total productive maintenance situation.

Some readers might argue that to identify the time to failure of a component, and then replace it even when it is not broken is nothing more than following the principles of preventive maintenance which are known and practised in the West. This may be true, but rarely does the workforce lead such activities. In western companies where preventive maintenance is implemented, the people who practise it come from the Plant Maintenance Department. They would be grossly under-resourced if they attempted to do this on anything like the scale that is normal in Japan. Only the workplace can provide the resource that QC Circle and Total Productive Maintenance-related activities demand. Such analysis may be conducted by the Maintenance Department or Industrial Engineering, but usually, the sheer volume of data which would need to be collected and processed by such off-line functions in the detail demanded would be beyond the resources of such departments. When collected by the workforce, the data are almost costless and the workers enjoy this form of involvement. Breakdowns are probably as much a frustration for them as they are to the Scheduling Department, as well as the managing director when he analyzes the factory costs.

It does not require much imagination to see how these ideas might be applied (see Table 5.1).

In Japan, it is estimated that over 80 per cent of all problem-solving requires nothing more than the application of the simple tools described here: frequency diagrams for both attribute and variable data. What could be simpler? But it doesn't happen.

Frequency diagrams for simple control

So far, this chapter has been limited to discussing and demonstrating the application of very simple techniques to identify causes and compare data. By using these basic techniques and without requiring mathematical skills, a small extension of the basic thinking allows the application of the tools for subsequent process control, and ensures that the gains of the improvement are sustained. Note that in every case described so far, the frequency curves exhibit a common characteristic. The curves all peter out into a short tail on either one or both sides of the average value. In the case of attribute data, there is only one tail if the average is close to zero, and two tails when the average number of the signal being counted is significantly higher. In the catheter bag example, it can be seen that this was the case for the third welding head. However, even when this is the case, with

Table 5.1. Applications for variable and attribute data

Problem	Type of data
Warehouse picking errors	Attribute
Telephone answering times	Variable or attribute
Customer complaints	Attribute
Debtors and creditors	Variable
Keyboard errors	Attribute
Order to delivery time	Variable
Product development	Variable and attribute
Wrong and late deliveries	Variable and attribute
Errors, breakdowns, faults	Variable and attribute

attribute data, the observer is usually more concerned with the outer tail than the inner tail (but not always, as will be seen in a moment).

In the case of variable data, the frequency diagram will always exhibit two tails, unless one has been deliberately cut off in some way, or when the process is subject to a specific constraint. These cases are relatively rare and can be ignored in this discussion. These tails are important in statistics and are also important in improvement projects and process control.

Consider the catheter bag case. Suppose that the group had managed to find the reasons why heads 2 and 3 were inferior to head 1, and that subsequent data collection had indicated that all three were exhibiting similar frequency curves. This exercise is called *process capability study*. Now, it would be desirable to hold the gains and ensure that the process was maintained at its higher level. Note that the curve for head A, which is similar to the curve in Figure 5.15 had one tail at about three occurrences per batch. Note also that the second or middle curve in the figure is a significantly different shape, even though the average number of faults is only slightly greater. Note also that, whereas in curve 1, three faults per batch were found on one occasion only during the sampling period, and that there was none worse, in the case of curve 2, three faults was a very frequent occurrence, as was four or even five. This observation can be put to good use for improvement control.

If an arbitrary line is put just in front of the three defects per sample level in Figure 5.15 we would expect, on average, if sampling is continued, for three defects to occur in a sample approximately

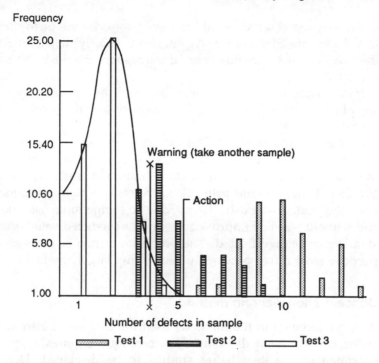

Figure 5.15 Faults per batch for effective improvement control

once in every 50 samples, provided that the process continues to behave as it is at present. However, if three faults occur, even though it may still be a random event, the procedure should be immediately to take another sample. If this also indicates three or even more faults, it is a fairly safe assumption that the process has deteriorated, because three will occur at random in a sample on average 1 in 50 times. This is a relatively rare event and the chart shows this.

Everybody knows instinctively that if a rare event is followed immediately by the same rare event, then something has almost certainly changed. If we could not do that instinctively, then magicians would not attract much interest. A good example, which almost exactly illustrates the case of the welding heads, is the card trick where one card – say the ace of spades – is dealt from the top of a well-shuffled pack. It had to be one of the 52, and it happened to be that one. No surprises so far. Just as with the three faults sample, also about 1 in 50. However, if the card is returned to the pack, shuffled and cut, and again, the ace of spades appears at the top, the observer would not even consider the possibility that it had happened by chance. Again, this is exactly the situation with the welding head. In this case, the question should be 'What has changed?'

Note again that all this was accomplished without resort to sampling tables, binomial or Poisson theories, just basic common sense!

In the case of attribute data, the reason why the outer tail is considered most important is because a move in that direction indicates that the situation is deteriorating. Clearly this is to be avoided. However, the principle of rare events applies equally to the other tail, if it exists. If, by chance, something has suddenly and without warning improved beyond its predicted value, then this should also be investigated. The process can then be made to do on purpose what it had previously been doing largely by luck.

Concentration diagram method

A novel variation in the methods used for analysis of attribute data is the concentration diagram. The technique requires a picture or specimen of the item being studied to be displayed. Defects or mistakes subsequently found on other items would then be marked on the sample or sketch. Sometimes the marks will produce a random pattern. Other times, clusters of marks build up in certain areas indicating a special cause at that point.

Case 4 Stitching faults (using concentration diagram method)

A garment factory was concerned about the number of stitching defects incurred in the make-up of men's underpants. The workers were involved in solving the problem and decided to use this method. They displayed a picture of a pair of pants on the wall in the work area. Each time a worker found a defect, its location on the garment was marked on the chart. After a few days it was noted that clusters had accumulated in certain areas (see Figure 5.16). Further study of the process in the areas highlighted indicated the cause and led to a remedy.

This method is used extensively in the car industry to identify clusters of dents or paint defects. It can also be used on documents, street plans to identify key accident spots, and many other applications. This is an extremely versatile and graphic technique.

Figure 5.16   Concentration diagram to show location of stitching faults

Variable data control

Variable data can be treated in much the same way as attribute data for the purpose of control, and the reasoning related to the tails can be applied. Usually, a shift of the data towards either tail is unwelcome. Consequently, the action and warning lines are placed at both extremes, as shown in Figure 5.17.

These limit lines can be calculated using statistical formulae (or a calculator) and in most examples familiar to the western manager this would be the case. However, as with all of the previous examples it is questionable whether it is necessary to go to such lengths, particularly if it means that only about 2 per cent of the payroll will understand the theory, and almost certainly develop rejection characteristics!

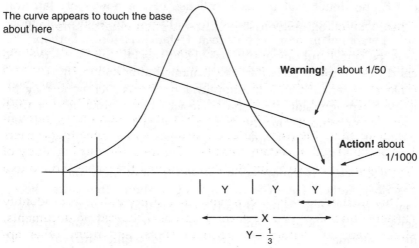

Figure 5.17   Variable data for control

If the curve is produced, and then, simply by eye, the point is marked where the curve appears to touch the base line; this would approximate to the point beyond which about 1 in 1,000 items or readings would go only by chance. It is a safe bet that when this does happen, the process can be regarded as having changed and a diagnosis should be made to discover why. If the distance from this point to the mean or average is divided by three, then at about two-thirds of this distance, items that go beyond will occur approximately on average about 1 in 50 times. This is precisely the same as with the attribute reasoning. Any two samples that go beyond this point will occur $1/50 \times 1/50 = 1/2500$, which is extremely unlikely – another very simple method of process control available to the most uneducated process worker to help make the work seem more meaningful.

Of course, all of these techniques are capable of considerable development, but why start at such levels? Surely, it makes sense to give employees simple techniques which they can use with confidence, understanding what they are doing before moving up the scale to more elaborate concepts, whose applications and able practitioners become rarer as further sophistication is introduced.

Moving up the scale

Treatment of the subject of data collection and analysis thus far is for universal application to enable everyone in an organization to become involved in decision-making based on facts. However, there can be no doubt that to make full use of the power of statistical concepts, an organization should invest in training some of its more able personnel in more sophisticated statistical tools. Perhaps the most powerful and universally-based statistical techniques is the $\bar{X}/R$ chart (the so-called Shewhart chart, named after its inventor).

Development towards the application of this technique may be made by progression from the basic variables techniques, or they may be introduced directly, but only, it is recommended, when applied by those sufficiently educated to understand the underlying theory.

The $\bar{X}/R$ chart is a more sophisticated form of the variables charts described earlier. The disadvantage is that the mathematical theory may be daunting for some; the advantage is that it is very much more sensitive than the crude methods so far described, and provides more information about the process in less time and will detect changes more quickly.

Using this technique instead of plotting individual items of data, successive items of 4, 5, 6, 7 or 8 items are averaged and it is the average of these which is plotted, not the individual. The chart on which these data are plotted is known as $\bar{X}$ chart or averages chart, $\bar{X}$ being the mathematical symbol for average.

On a separate chart, the range between the highest and lowest value in the sample items is plotted. For example, suppose a control chart is being constructed for recording variations in the temperature of a room, and the average chart based on samples of four consecutive readings

$$28.4°C$$
$$28.2°C$$
$$28.0°C$$
$$28.2°C$$

Average   28.2°C

On the average chart 28.2°C would be plotted.

The largest to smallest range is:

$$28.4 - 28.0 = 0.4°C$$

This would be plotted on a separate chart known as the R or range chart, hence the term $\bar{X}/R$ chart.

Data plotted on a $\bar{X}/R$ chart appear in Figure 5.18.

In many Japanese companies even the financial data used in profit and loss accounts are plotted on this type of chart for control purposes. The limit lines are calculated from formulae derived from estimates involving the standard deviation of the samples used to construct the chart. While the theory behind these calculations may require some thought, the calculations to produce the action lines are basic and, of course, with the use of software such as JUSE-QCAS and others, even that chore has been eliminated. All that is necessary is to input the data.

Case 5 The cracked bed

A medium-sized company, employing some 400 people in the automotive components industry, decided to experiment with the implementation of $\bar{X}/R$ control charts in the manufacture of gudgeon pins, the small cylindrical components located in a piston to provide a bearing for the rod which connects the piston to the crank shaft. The gudgeon pin is a high-precision component and is required to

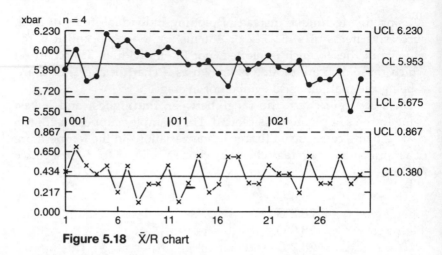

Figure 5.18 X̄/R chart

work in an exacting environment involving high levels of stress and change of temperature and the need for stable physical properties. Nevertheless, while these demands required the very highest levels of machinery capability at the final stages of production, surprisingly wide latitudes of dimensional accuracy were tolerated in the early production processes. These inaccuracies were not thought to be important prior to the heat treatment process as it was considered that, at this stage, scale and other surface problems were such that considerable grinding would be necessary afterwards, at which time the variations could be removed.

The first experiment was conducted on a 3″ Butterworth Semi Automatic Lathe. This machine was selected because it had a very slow cycle time, and as a first operation machine tool was not very accurate, and even with the wide limits of tolerance at this stage struggled to maintain requirements and required constant checking. In order to set up the parameters on the control chart, ten consecutive samples of four items were selected from the process. Care was taken to ensure that none of the settings on the machine was altered and that operations were continuous with consistent raw material. As a bar feed automatic, this meant ensuring that the bar of raw material would not run out and require replacement during the sample period. This is important when setting up the basic control parameters.

Measurements were taken on the items selected and the action and warning limits plotted on both the average and range charts. Several of the readings were outside the control lines. This did not seem to make sense. If the lines were constructed from the data, how could the data be outside the lines themselves? At first it was thought that some error had been made in the calculations. So these were checked several times, as were the theory and the measurements of the components. Then it was realized that the formula used to construct the diagram was based on the assumption that the data were distributed according to the laws of the normal distribution for process variables. When the averages of the samples of four were arranged in histogram form it was found that this was not the case. The data were all over the place and did not appear to conform to any distribution.

The engineer consulted the setters of the machines as well as the operators. Many theories were suggested to explain why this should be the case. The most popular theories are shown in Figure 5.19.

The 'cracked bed' suggestion was more than a theory. The machine had been purchased secondhand and the setters knew that the machine bed was cracked. When asked why they hadn't volunteered this information, the reply was: 'No one ever asked'.

The machine bed was repaired by the toolroom. Again, samples were taken and still the results behaved abnormally, but were better than before. However, while the engineer was standing by the machine, one of the operators checked a component and decided to adjust the size. What happened was interesting and to follow what

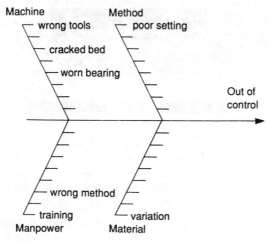

Figure 5.19 Fishbone diagram

happened it is necessary to understand a little more of the process. Figure 5.20 shows the machine, the component and the dimension being checked.

The tool was held in the tool holder by an allen screw. The operator slackened the screw, tapped the tool lightly with a mallet, measured the next component, then left the machine. At the same time, it was noticed that the surface finish on the components was very irregular. When the tool was inspected, it was noted that it had been reground to bizarre dimensions. Nothing was said, but the machine was then observed over a number of days and across shifts. It was noted that the shape of the cutting tool varied considerably, depending on which setter did the regrinding. It was obvious that the tool setting required a better design of adjustment, and that the tool shape had to be standardized in accordance with best practice. Both problems were solved simultaneously. A new tool holder was purchased with a micrometer adjustment eliminating the need for the mallet. The tools themselves, which were of hardened steel, were replaced by a new design which used replaceable, pre-ground carbide tips. This ensured the use of correct tool-cutting angles and foolproofed against

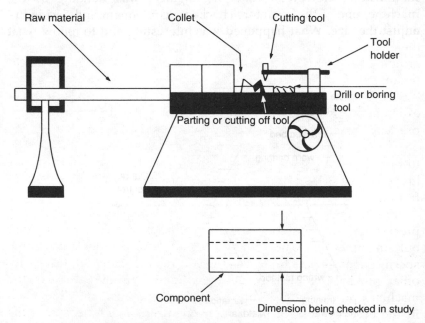

Figure 5.20 The machine tool

unauthorized experimentation. When these changes were introduced there was a spectacular improvement in the results. Not only did the machine behave precisely to the rules of statistical theory, but the variation was so small that it was debatable whether it was necessary to do any form of in-process inspection let alone use the $\bar{X}$/R chart concept.

However, the concept was used, and in fact applied to the entire line. The setters and operators who had originally viewed the whole exercise with great suspicion – and at the start with some barely concealed amusement – changed to being interested and impressed, then finally not only to being enthusiastic, but also wanting to use the techniques themselves. There was a great deal of difficulty experienced in attempting to provide an understanding of the basics of $\bar{X}$/R, and in the end, the attempt was abandoned. Instead, the basic approach outlined above was introduced. The concepts were readily understood by everyone, and it was not long before frequency diagram curves were appearing for all sorts of measures. One setter used the concept to prove that one brand of drill lasted 20 per cent longer than its competitors and required fewer regrinds. Eventually, either $\bar{X}$/R charts, attribute charts or the simplified charts were established on all key operations in the plant. In some cases – and this included the lathe example above – the improvements eliminated the need for a number of operations. In the case of the 3″ lathe the new accuracy eliminated the need for two grinding operations before heat treatment and one grinding post-heat treatment.

Shortly afterwards, the company entered into a major capital expenditure programme in order to renew all of its finishing high-precision operations, measurements and production methods. The object was to put severe pressure on the competition and be able to respond to the growing demands of the automotive industry for higher levels of performance from its products and to competition from Japan.

Prior to and during the period of implementation of statistical process control, the company had purchased a variety of plant but on an *ad hoc* basis, without much control and from vague specifications. Apart from like for like replacements, almost every other purchase resulted in disappointment. Virtually none of the machines purchased lived up to their expectations, and all resulted in the excessive use of production engineering time to obtain the required results.

The engineer who had been responsible for the introduction of statistical process control decided to use this method to develop a new product acceptance sampling procedure, in which the statistical process capability was established in the new plant at the suppliers' premises prior to shipment. On satisfactory testing, a proportion of the purchase price was paid. The tests were then repeated after satisfactory installation at the plant. A further proportion was paid. The final payment followed six months later when the product had proved that it was capable of maintaining its contracted performance to the satisfaction of the specification. All of this happened several years ago, before statistical process control became popular in the West. The plant which was purchased on this basis was still giving satisfactory performance several years later.

Many companies reluctantly pay lip-service to statistical process control because they are forced to do so by their customers. In many cases they do not understand it, and only do what they are made to do. This is unfortunate because statistical process control probably offers the most powerful means available for cost reduction and continuous incremental improvement, if it is used properly. If it is used by the direct employees or operators and supported by suitable software, then the results could, in time, reach Japanese levels.

6 Quality improvement – the human factor

We are going to win and the industrial West is going to lose out; there's not much you can do about it because the reasons for your failure are within yourselves.

Your firms are built on the Taylor Model. Even worse, so are your heads. With your bosses doing the thinking while the workers wield the screwdrivers, you're convinced deep down that this is the right way to run a business. For you the essence of management is getting the ideas out of the heads of the bosses and into the hands of labour.

We are beyond the Taylor Model. Business, we know, is now so complex and difficult, the survival of firms so hazardous in an environment increasingly unpredictable, competitive and fraught with danger, that their continued existence depends on the day-to-day mobilization of every ounce of intelligence.

Konosuke Matsushita

This chapter covers all aspects of employee roles and relationships with a focus on the problems of western-style organization and how a TQ organization can solve them. It covers:

- Professional specialization as a problem in business process management
- Problem-solving skills for project by project improvement
- On the job training
- Short-termism vs. lifetime employment
- The problems of Taylorism and the division of labour
- The role of the chief executive

The late Professor Ishikawa, regarded in Japan as the 'father of QC Circles', continually emphasized his belief that 'Total Quality begins and ends with education.' Education is a word seldom used in our industrial companies, but most have training departments. Training is directly skills-related, but education is a people-building concept. It is only through education that people can be developed to make good decisions, and it is only through education that the full benefits of people-based philosophies such as Total Quality can be achieved.

Getting results from people

In an earlier chapter it was suggested that quality-related costs are likely to amount to a minimum of 20 per cent of turnover at the commencement of the introduction of Total Quality. It is these costs that provide an opportunity to introduce Total Quality and simultaneously recover the investment.

Quality-related costs occur in all departments and at all levels; it is necessary to identify these at an early stage. However, not all key quality improvement opportunities are expressed in financial terms, although they will have a financial effect, for example, the time to develop, produce and deliver new products, engineering change notes, labour turnover, failed product launch, security, safety, etc. The improvement process is concerned with all of these. In fact, it is concerned with everything that could be described as a perceived inferior level of performance. Such information may have been obtained from benchmarking against best practices.

Project identification can be carried out by any group at any level within an organization. The problems identified by different groups will vary depending upon experience. Generally, the higher the level of group within the organization, the higher will be the level of problem identified. For example, a board of directors will be concerned with such problems as cash flow, low sales, increasing direct costs, higher overheads, excess costs on new investments, low yields, prior franchise by competitors, quality of recruiting, etc. In an office, problems will include such features as lack of space, wrong information, too much bureaucracy, poor communication, late deliveries, absenteeism, untrained staff, dissatisfied customers, queues, mistakes, poor software, unreliable photocopiers, slow computer hardware, and so on. All of these problems, at whatever level, are important to the people at that level, and ultimately, to the organization as a whole.

The objective of Total Quality is to create an organization where everyone is working to make that organization the best in its field. To do this requires empowering the people and giving them the opportunity to tackle the problems they recognize and have the skills to solve.

Problems in organizations can be divided into three distinct categories:

1. Problems within the scope of those who may be affected.
2. Problems partially within their scope.
3. Problems outside their scope.

As a general rule, problems in category 1 will either be major and endemic in the organisation as a whole, for example, high inventory, or they may be relatively small but plentiful, the reason being that the latter problems are either regarded by higher levels of management as being too small or trivial to be worth the trouble to solve, or in the case of the former, require too much resource or time to tackle them while simultaneously carrying out line duties. If the full range of potential problems in this category were to be arranged in column graph format, the result would probably look like Figure 6.1.

It can be seen that the middle-range problems will usually have been dealt with. The reason for this is that those responsible will have recognized those problems that are within their scope and in all probability the skills were available to tackle them without disruption to other activities.

At managerial levels, by far the most numerous and costly problems are likely to be found in the 'partially within scope' group. Problems of this type are in abundance in western organizations for two reasons: (1) there is no one group, section or department which sees them as their problems; (2) without formal, Total Quality, project by

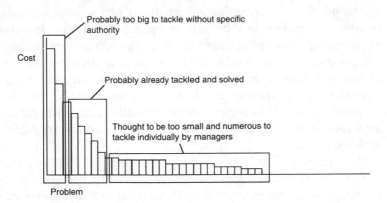

Figure 6.1 Typical range of problems

project improvement activities, no structure exists to identify, analyze and solve such problems on a regular basis.

In the absence of organized, project by project improvement activities, problems in category 3 will also remain unsolved since there will be no individual responsible to identify those who could deal with such problems.

Against this background, it is not surprising that so many problems remain unsolved and that the potential offered by project by project improvement is so high.

Professional specialization is another or perhaps the major reason for the existence of so many problems of this type. Short Bros, with a payroll of 8,500 people, identified some 24,000 problems in their first year or so of implementing Total Quality. This does not imply that Short Bros are any worse than any other company. On the contrary, Shorts are probably one of the most professional companies in Europe in their field. It simply means that Shorts are very good at problem identification. The fact that they are on track to save £15 million in one year indicates that they also have become expert in solving them as well!

Professional specialization

'Professional specialization' has become endemic in the United Kingdom. The concept was imported from the United States in the 1950s. 'Professional specialization' is a direct and natural development from the division of labour concept originated by Frederick W. Taylor. Division of labour led to deskilling and created the need for functional specialisms such as production engineering, work study, training, industrial engineering, personnel, industrial relations, etc. The key benefit of specialization results from the opportunity afforded to those assigned to such groups to study and acquire great depth of skill and knowledge in their respective areas of management science. This provides a considerable advantage over the earlier system in which the foreman or supervisor was required to be as skilled as possible in all areas, without offering any competition to the highly trained experts who have since divided up his job.

The downside of this development lies in the tendency for professionally trained groups to coalesce into organizations such as the professional institutions. These exist to further and promote the interests of their members. This is good in some respects, but the members of such 'professions' tend to develop their own jargon and methods, which may be incomprehensible to others. Some of this tendency is reasonable, but much is not and can result in unwittingly creating protective barriers. All this is destructive to business organizations because it can result in designers talking to designers, marketing talking to marketing, sales talking to sales and finance talking to finance. There exists no company-wide language, only specialist language.

The problem also impinges on loyalties. A young graduate entering industry will have been forced to identify a 'career' in a specialist activity in all but exceptional industries, notably banking. The graduate will not necessarily envisage a lifetime in one company, but may envisage a lifetime in a chosen 'profession'. In fact, as a result of American influence in the 1950s, the new graduate will be encouraged *not* to stay in one company but to move from company to company, in the expectation of getting a higher salary and gaining experience and seniority along the way. The process has some merit, but it also contributes to the problems of professional specialization. As a result, a greater sense of loyalty to the 'profession' is developed other than to the current employer. This process results in very strong vertical fibres of organization but extremely weak horizontal fibres. Since processes tend to progress horizontally it means that no one owns the process (see Figure 6.2). In manufacturing the designer may receive little or no information from market research. And any information that is given may be in an incomprehensible form. The designer therefore may produce something to which the potential customer is completely indifferent. Under such regimes, the problem

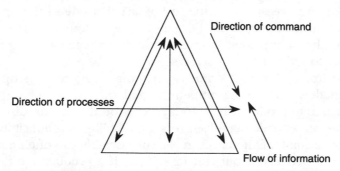

Figure 6.2   Horizontal vs vertical fibres of an organization

will be made worse by the fact that the designer is probably bewitched by the eloquence of the technology, which may then be foisted onto an indifferent market.

It is quite likely that it was precisely this effect that turned the fortunes of the then British Motor Corporation. The Morris 1000 in its day was the most successful car ever produced in Britain in terms of both popularity and reliability. Then, at the same time as Nissan, under the Datsun label, were introducing cars with radios, BMC launched the 1100 series with its transverse engine and hydroelastic suspension. Technically, these achievements may have been impressive, but the customers liked the idea of the radio. They couldn't understand hydroelastic suspension anyway, and the car didn't feel any different. When it started to go wrong because of the unnecessary complexity, all was lost.

The designer may also design something that is either impossible or unnecessarily difficult to produce or assemble: a perfect product that is almost perfectly impossible to produce. The cost of engineering changes experienced by Ford (described in Chapter 3), in comparison to Mazda and Toyota, were no exception. It is typical of many western companies. And the problem is not restricted to manufacturing. The same thing happens in chemicals and pharmaceutical industries. There have been many examples where processes which worked well in the laboratory could not be repeated under manufacturing conditions, with often catastrophic results. Problems like this have closed down companies. One of the most common and expensive problems in design or project engineering companies is the cost of designing something the customer does not want, because the original specification was vague.

The problem also extends to assembly. There is an old story in the motor industry of the assembly line that did not start up one morning. The reason was due to the fact that one of the operators had not turned up for work. Because two of his fingers were missing, he was the only person who could reach between the engine and gearbox to tighten certain screws! This may be a sick joke, but it is not far from the truth. Motor car manufacturers today strip down new models from their competitors and then reassemble them to measure the producibility. Today, one of the major differences between automobile manufacturers' profitability is producibility and ease of assembly. Differences in ease of assembly can often make the difference between profit and loss. Also, if a product is difficult to assemble on the line, it will be even more difficult for less skilled people to maintain or repair. This will affect the whole life, cost and reputation in the marketplace.

After assembly comes packing and shipping. Products are often designed to perfection, manufactured and assembled with care and then spoiled because the packing is inferior. This is as much the responsibility of design as the product itself. Minolta Cameras in Japan have a test laboratory in which every possible test is carried out on packaging, including humidity, sand and drop tests to ensure the quality of delivery. If a product is damaged on arrival, it reflects as much on the manufacturer as it does on the distributor.

Finally, comes the link between design and customer care. Most readers will be familiar with pocket calculators, personal computers and hi-fi systems. It is remarkable how often the installation and instruction manuals for products like these are totally unintelligible to the user. They may well be written by someone with a high IQ who assumes that the customer is equally intelligent. Total Quality organizations recognize these problems, as well as the relationships between finance, cost control, personnel, maintenance, purchasing and line management. When these interactions are taken into account it is not surprising that other organizations have problems. But they can be dealt with highly effectively. Organizations which have addressed the problem have found that, in many cases, the remedies have been surprisingly simple. Japan experienced these problems in the 1950s and early 1960s but, as with so many other management problems, they have found a solution. In Japan, professional specialization is avoided, although the Japanese themselves admit that the problem is always potentially there and does exist to some extent.

To get round the problem of professional specialization, Japanese companies have developed a simple method that not only reduces the likelihood of cross-boundary problems experienced by their western competitors, but has the advantage of ensuring the widest possible application of skills, which, while developed for one specialist activity, can equally be used in others, e.g. statistical quality control techniques. These were first developed by Dr Walter Shewhart to elevate the concept of quality control from the mere segregation of parts into good and bad, to the prevention of defects. The statistical techniques he developed were very powerful, but in the West people on the shopfloor found the sophistication of the mathematics somewhat daunting and hence the techniques have never been used to best effect. In Japan not only are the techniques fully employed on production processes, they are also used throughout the organization in marketing, finance, sales, personnel, research and development, and so forth. This is because Japanese graduates do not specialize in one activity. When Japanese graduates leave university or senior high school they begin a career development programme which will go on for most of their working life.

Initially, they are assigned to a department. The assignment may well be unrelated to the graduate's career goal or demonstrated capability, because this will be the beginning of a process which is intended to develop the graduate as a 'company' employee. At an early stage, the new employee will almost certainly be posted to an activity directly related to the marketplace. This might include dealerships, distribution, sales, marketing or market research. During this period, the new recruit will receive considerable education in the company's products and market competitors, company goals and aspirations, in addition to the activities of the department in question. On-the-job training is highly organized in Japanese companies and new recruits are also expected to participate in self-improvement programmes in special skills. And if they are ambitious, most of them do. These will invariably include basic, intermediate and advanced courses in statistical techniques and encouragement to make decisions based on facts.

Problem-solving skills, teamwork and the basics of scientific management feature in virtually all training programmes in Japan.

Employees move from department to department, function to function as part of their career progression. They may be 35 years old before this process has been completed, and the move is made to a senior position. By this time, the employee will be totally conversant with all company activities, the role of every department and their organization in every detail. Work colleagues will be mostly of a similar age and intake, but importantly, the function in which they work will be totally irrelevant to this relationship because they will also have been employed in similar duties. This difference between Japanese and western-style organizations is of great importance and provides the Japanese with a significant advantage which is not easily overcome. With this approach, it is easy for the Japanese to develop cross-functional teamwork because everyone has the same knowledge base. The Japanese designer will be far less likely to design something the customer does not want, because it is unlikely that the designer will be employed in design until he or she has worked in both market research and in operations. He or she will probably also have been acquainted with finance and can then communicate easily with the most important customers and suppliers. The Japanese designer is most unlikely to design something which cannot be made because he or she will be as acquainted with production as those who work there.

Incidentally, this approach is not outside the experience of western industry. The clearing banks operate in this way. Years ago, all new bank employees at any level of academic ability would begin their careers as cashiers. What better way to find out who the customers are and develop a customer-first mentality. Military organizations also recognize the value of starting at the bottom, and both officers and NCOs move around a wide range of specializations in the course of their careers. There are also many pay-related inducements to learn special skills parallel to the Japanese approach. Many western companies would complain that this policy is not applicable to them because their own up-and-coming executives would not stay with the company long enough for the concept to be effective and, in any case, surely it is better to allow people to move from company to company to gain experience. In the view of the author this is a flawed argument. While some cross-fertilization inevitably does take place by this method, it may not follow that what is learned represents best or even good practice. All it means is that the differences are 'different', they're not necessarily better!

The supposed (but not scientifically proven) advantages of encouraging the concept of the 'butterfly executive' must be weighed against the following:

1. Companies are reluctant to invest in education and training because they do not want to train the future employees of their competitors. In the end, no one trains or educates anybody. The result: mass mediocrity in western management.
2. There is a tendency towards short-termism at all levels, e.g. board of directors – individuals may be attracted to short-term strategies which 'look good' for the next year or two, but which could be disastrous in the long run. The results can be included in a personal portfolio for the next employer. Their replacement will have to pick up the pieces and the cycle begins all over again. The payroll will remain unconvinced by any top-level initiatives or drives because they know that within 2–3 years just about all of the directors who made the commitment will have left. The replacements will almost certainly make different commitments;

they will want to impose their own style. This problem applies even more directly to the chief executive, the consequence being a cyclical organization rather than a progressive one (see Figure 6.3).

3. The long-term future of the organization is of little consequence to anyone other than those locked into a pension scheme. Nowadays, with transferable pensions, even this consideration has largely disappeared. At the rate at which companies are bought, sold and carved up, it is surprising there is any loyalty left at all.

This is a serious problem – perhaps the most serious problem – because unless some solution is found, it will be impossible to introduce the concepts described in this book with any guarantee of long-term success. Many programmes have already failed for no other reason.

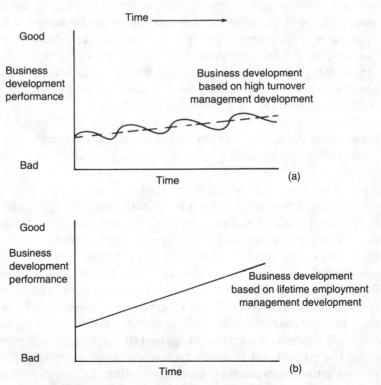

Figure 6.3 Business development based on high turnover vs lifetime employment of managers

How can western industry encourage its people not to move on, but to regard the business as a life-time career? Again, the Japanese have a remedy. They are very aware of the importance of this difference between themselves and western companies and therefore take measures to reduce the likelihood of erosion into western habits.

Lifetime employment in Japan may be a cultural characteristic, but it is not a permanent one. And because the Japanese regard the concept as superior to western short-termism, they employ means to protect the effect. The main inducement is money.

In Japanese companies, new employees at all levels start at a basic level of pay commensurate with their academic background and the expectations of the business. Further increases are incremental, based on years of service, profitability of the company and special attainments. This progression is continuous, regardless of age or department in which they are employed. It is obviously in everyone's interests to increase profitability. If the employee were subsequently to leave the company and seek employment elsewhere, he or she would almost certainly take a drop in pay because the upper management of the new employer would be sensitive to the fact that existing employees, given their involvement in intensive and continuous improvement activities and the close relationships they have developed, would be deeply resentful if an outsider gained even a salary equal to theirs, let alone a higher one. And, if a newcomer takes a lower salary, they would be suspicious as to why he or she had moved on.

Japanese managements also recognize that in a society where lifetime employment has become the norm, it is important to attract the best people. This is a tough assignment if hiring and firing is not an option. Ideally, the leading Japanese companies seek to cream off the top of the labour market. In a lifetime environment this means school-leavers and university graduates. It also means that the company must attempt to influence both parents and the schools. No one will encourage their young people to join a company that has a reputation for hiring and firing, or not looking after its employees. This is one of the key reasons why Japanese companies seek good relationships with the unions. The social programme in a Japanese company and the reputation it acquires as being a good employer is almost as important in the eyes of the manager as its reputation in the marketplace. The goal of attracting the cream in the employment marketplace is a key competitive challenge in Japan. It is not surprising, therefore, that every Japanese manager is conscious of the importance of listening to the employees' suggestions, providing opportunities for participation in Quality Control Circle activities, self-development programmes and anything that will build on the loyalty and sense of community which can be developed. This consciousness extends to part-time employees as well, and most companies give their part-timers the opportunity of participating in Quality Control Circles.

What can western companies do to fight back? There can be no quick fix to reach the ultimate situation, but fortunately very effective partial remedies have been developed. The most important is the concept of 'process chain management'. This is based on Professor Kaoru Ishikawa's observation that each individual or each department is the customer or supplier to the next. This idea has been developed further and is expressed by the Juran Institute as the 'Triple Role'. This adds to the customer/supplier concept, that each person in the chain is also a 'processor' (see Figure 6.4), i.e. while all individuals will see themselves as being a 'processor', in the eyes of the supplier they will be seen as a 'customer', and in the eyes of the customer as a supplier. Hence, everyone will be simultaneously 'supplier', 'processor' and 'customer'. The key questions then will be: (1) Do I meet the requirements of my customer or user? And (2) Have I discussed my needs with my suppliers so that they appreciate my situation?

Since everyone has a wide range of suppliers and customers, the task of answering these questions, even in a small organization, will be onerous. However, while everyone will have a wide range of both suppliers and customers they are not all equally important. The Pareto principle is almost certain to apply: i.e. about 20 per cent of the interactions will be critical to performance achievement. If this 20 per cent can be identified, then some major improvements can be made for a relatively small amount of effort. However, even with this approach, dealing with all interactions will still be demanding on the resources of a busy organization, so the problem must be simplified further, and the activities themselves subject to Pareto analysis.

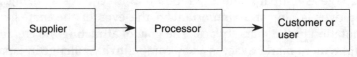

Figure 6.4 The 'triple role'

First, the major process chains of the business must be identified. These will include such processes as product development and planning, profit and loss forecasting, cost estimating, and new business prospecting, etc. In some cases the process chains will be quite long, involving several different activities and functions. Only a proportion of the process in the chain will be critical to the performance of the process and these may be identified subjectively. The target will be to identify about five key process elements (see Figure 6.5).

Figure 6.5 Key process elements

For each key process element individuals will be selected to form a team. It will then be the responsibility of the team to optimize the output of the process chain. This will require skills in identifying the key causes of low performance, testing theories of causes, implementing improvements and monitoring results. This method is being introduced into a number of western companies with impressive results.

Organizationally, it has been found that there will be occasions when the changes or improvements will be beyond the capability of the team, or alternatively require the cooperation of someone outside the team. In order to facilitate this, each process chain team may have a sponsor at a higher level of organization, preferably high enough to sanction the requirements. Major gains are being made via this approach and it looks likely to develop throughout industry in the future. Process chain management is an excellent method for tackling and solving the problems identified under the partially group solvable category. Western companies are already saving millions of pounds through the adoption of this approach. But of course, it doesn't address the problem of short-termism and all of its inherent risks.

A remedy for short-termism

Short-termism comes about when people think they would be better off elsewhere by moving around. People cannot be prevented from doing this and even in Japan it occurs to some extent. In fact, recently, it has been said that moving from company to company in Japan is on the increase and a cause of worry. Western companies are also impacting on Japan by offering very attractive salaries to Japanese executives in order to buy their expertise. However, many Japanese are reluctant to make such a move even for the highest salaries because they know that once they have fallen for the temptation it will be very difficult for them to return to their own society and they do not have much confidence in the westerners' promises of a long-term career.

Means by which short-termism can be discouraged include:

- Salaries related to length of service.
- Share option schemes at all levels.
- Profit-sharing schemes for all employees.
- Long-term career development at all levels including Quality Control Circle activities for direct employees.
- Merit pay for company-authorized self-education and for on-the-job training.
- Promotion of the company as a good employer.
- Influence in universities, polytechnics, colleges and schools.
- Social activities.
- Long-service award schemes, social support for retired personnel including directors.
- Visible support for local organizations and charities.
- Involvement in local affairs in the vicinity of the company.
- Encourage the City to alter its financial methods to encourage long-termism.

The role of Quality Circles

It is now well known in the West that Japanese companies make extensive use of the Quality Control Circle concept. Perhaps it is less well known that the QC Circle is the principle by which management maintains links with the workforce.

Japanese Quality Control Circle programmes are misunderstood in western organizations and there is a widespread view in the West that the concept has been discredited. Most of the evidence would support this view. After all, at least 90 per cent of all attempts to introduce Quality Control Circles in the United Kingdom since around 1983/4 have failed, but interestingly some of the earlier initiatives have survived. But even many of the survivors are pale imitations of their Japanese equivalent. Many observers attribute this apparent difference to cultural factors and believe that the failure of circles in the West provides evidence to support this view. Of course, they may well be right and so far no one has proved otherwise. However, in view of the obvious potential of Japanese Quality Control Circles and their impact on a company's performance, the West should not dismiss the concept too easily.

In Japan today, a very significant part of the power of Total Quality is focused through Quality Control Circles. These groups are not simply involved in solving the myriad of small problems individually which may be meaningless as a factor influencing a company's performance. This is what many westerners think, but they have not looked closely enough. The philosophy behind Quality Control Circles is more profound than many western people appreciate. We are prepared to believe that the best ideas emanate from the United States and particularly from the Harvard Business School, but somehow find it difficult to accept the possibility that equally good ideas may and do originate in Japan. Japanese management, and its national supportive infrastructures in organizations such as the Japanese Union of Scientists and Engineers, expend considerable amounts of time and money encouraging, educating and developing Quality Control Circle activities. If Japanese managers go to these lengths on something as apparently simple and 'meaningless' as Quality Control Circles, one can be sure that there is something important to be learned. No Japanese manager wastes time on irrelevancies, so the West should look again and look more closely. What will be discovered is that circles are not just problem-solving groups. The Quality Control Circle concept represents a totally new approach to managing people, people building and business development.

Originally conceived by Professor Kaoru Ishikawa, Quality Control Circle activities in Japan were initiated in 1962. The first nine recorded Quality Control Circles were formed at the Nippon Wireless and Telegraph company. In the same year more than thirty-five other companies followed suit. These circles were phenomenally successful, and the concept very soon began to sweep through Japan. They were started in the Toyota Motor Corporation in 1965. Of course, this development was considerably at variance with what happened subsequently in the United States and in Europe. In these cases, the Quality Control Circle concept also swept through the various countries in the late 1970s and early 1980s, but lasted in the main for some 5–6 years and then waned. In France, the organization which led the Quality Control Circle movement there was disbanded in the late 1980s. It would be easy to write off this experience as being nothing more than the typical lifecycle of a fad, and the reason why Japanese experience was different is because the Japanese are in some way 'different'. Possibly. But even if this were true – and it is doubtful – the fact remains that unless the West can come up with an alternative approach which equals or surpasses the power of Quality Control Circles or its several derivatives, then it will never be able to compete.

Perhaps it would be a good idea to take another look at Quality Control Circles.

Professor Ishikawa postulated the idea of Quality Control Circles because post-war Japan was beginning to experience precisely the same industrial relations problems that are so familiar in the West. This is not surprising because not only did the Japanese absorb the ideas of Drs Deming and Juran, they also copied American-style management.

American-style management was new to the Japanese in the 1950s and was based on the principles of mass or flow production. (This management concept was also being introduced into the United Kingdom at about the same time. It is interesting that while the approach was vastly different from the existing British style, there is no evidence that there was any debate as to whether the approach would be culturally acceptable to British workers.) The system had profound dehumanizing implications. So it is paradoxical that with the possibility of introducing Japanese management concepts which improve the acceptability of work, we debate and agonize about whether the concepts are culturally acceptable. In the late 1940s executives from Toyota, Nissan and other major Japanese manufacturing companies visited the United States. They went to the Ford Motor Company, General Motors and elsewhere to study American-style management. Just as in the United Kingdom, the Japanese implemented what they saw without challenge.

Prior to this period, just as in the United Kingdom, the Japanese used the craftsmanship concept, in which everyone is the expert in his or her own job, and a craftsman by definition is responsible for the quality of the work he or she produces. The foreman or supervisor is the main link between management and worker. He is well regarded by both and the main source of communication between them (See Figure 6.6). He is responsible for the discipline of the group, for skills development and provides social support.

The automotive industries in both Japan and the United Kingdom were the first in each country to break with this tradition in order to set up flow-line American-style production systems. In these systems, jobs are broken down into their smallest elements and all problem-solving passed to on-line specialists who are expected to solve all problems. No one asks the worker anything. No one involves the worker in anything. All that is required is the mindless repetition of tasks at a relentless pace, shift after shift, week after week. Socially, this process is close to intolerable and life on the assembly line became a living hell.

At the Nissan factory in Tokyo, the system broke down in 1959. In fact, throughout the late 1950s industrial relations in Japan were deteriorating at an alarming rate. The same thing was happening in the United Kingdom and in the United States, but there was an important difference. In both countries the economy was going through an unprecedented boom. Companies could sell everything they could make. Unfortunately, when that happens quality becomes irrelevant. Productivity dominates everything. Mass production techniques provide high volume at low cost. This in turn produces high profits and high profits produce high wages. Consequently, while the quality of life at work was plummeting and dehumanization becoming complete, wages were rocketing in compensation.

In Japan things were different. Mass production was implemented in Japan, but the Japanese could not sell what they were producing. Their plants were less efficient, machinery older and they had a world-wide reputation for making junk. Therefore the worker could not be compensated with higher pay, the profits were not there to

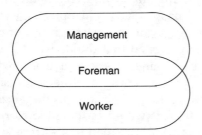

Figure 6.6 The craftsmanship relationship

allow it. And so the workers rebelled. At Nissan things got so bad that in 1959 the managers barricaded themselves into the factory for 47 days in fear of their lives.

Professor Ishikawa postulated that the American system of management was at fault and that it was alien to Japanese culture. (It was probably also alien to British culture as well as to American or indeed any culture.) Management under regimes developed from the mass production concept are an affrontery to human dignity. But, while the Japanese began to challenge American-style management, Britain began to dig in deeper. Concepts, it was postulated, that proved successful on the production line would work elsewhere. In fact, advocates of this approach argued that the techniques could work anywhere. Whether in offices, hospitals, banks or schools, the craftsmanship approach was rejected and the battery hen system introduced.

Prior to its development in the automotive industry, Frederick W. Taylor had postulated that all work could be broken down into its smallest elements and therefore deskilled. Taylor argued that by doing so, workers could be provided with the minimum of training, while managers and specialists should assume the responsibility for problem-solving. Thus began the science of work study, and later its evolution into organization and methods. From its roots in flow-line production, Taylorism spread in the West into offices, hospitals and by the mid-1960s could be found in every work environment. All work was reduced to the mindless and relentless repetition of soul-destroying monotony.

Meanwhile, in Japan, the opposite was happening. Having challenged Taylorism, Professor Ishikawa suggested that it might be possible to develop a new model. He proposed combining the benefits of craftsmanship with the benefits of Taylorism to produce a concept of work which avoided the disadvantages of both. In effect, Professor Ishikawa was postulating that while craftsmanship was uneconomical on an individual basis, and could not compete with Taylorism, it was possible to bring Taylorism back to groups of people rather than to individuals. He suggested that the division of labour and the breakdown of tasks be retained because it was obviously effective. But if small groups of workers under the leadership of their foreman or supervisor were trained to identify, analyze and solve work-related problems, then it would be possible to recover the craftsmanship mentality. As soon as experiments were started, Professor Ishikawa's theory was proved to be correct.

The small groups, called Quality Control Circles, were immediately successful, as indeed they have been in the West. Eventually, the adoption of Quality Control Circles in Japan revolutionized the whole approach to work there. The circle progressed from initially being involved in problem-solving to work improvement and then, with the essence of craftsmanship, developed to manage whole sections of plant as self-supervising work groups. Today, teams of circle workers are treated with great respect in Japan. Education goes far beyond simple problem-solving and extends where possible to include sophisticated statistical tools which are unknown in western companies even among technical specialists.

Total Productive Maintenance (TPM) is a concept that has grown directly out of Quality Control Circle activities. Through TPM, workers collect data on plant or process, breakdowns and other stoppages with the object of maximizing plant 'uptime' (a term referring to the actual time that specific units of plant are in good working order and available for use). The results are astonishing. Queuing theory, developed by operational research scientist and popular in the West, indicates that plant availability times in excess of 80 per cent are virtually unattainable if arrivals of product are in any way intermittent, without running the risk of alarming queues and therefore work in progress building up. Incredibly, with plant uptime of 94 per cent or thereabouts, Japanese companies are running near zero inventory.

However impressive these statistics may be, they still do not convey the essence of Quality Control Circles. Fundamentally, Quality Control Circles exist to break down all vestiges of Taylorism, but it is impossible for Quality Control Circles to exist in isolation or where Taylorism exists at higher levels. It is precisely this that is preventing the full development of Quality Control Circles in the West.

It is the author's hypothesis that the fundamental reason why circles are not developing properly in the West has nothing to do with cultural differences between the West and Japan. On the contrary, it could be argued that Quality Control Circles should flourish at least as well in the West, given the chances to do so. The main reason according to this hypothesis why circles do not flourish is because western managers refuse to abandon Taylorism for fear of loss of control, even though it has only been part of our culture for three to four decades. The Japanese abandoned Taylorism before it took hold. In Britain Taylorism has now been entrenched for some forty years.

Taylorism doesn't just affect the direct employee, it is the ultimate form of autocratic management, which starts from the top and then permeates down through organizations to their roots. It is a power-driven concept which at its worst represents pure theory 'x'-style management in which all employees – even managers – are regarded as lazy, indolent and work-shy. Therefore all performance must be achieved through threats and fear. Every action produces an equal and opposite reaction (Newton's second law). The reaction of the unions has been obvious, but the same applies to management. Managers in a pure theory 'x', Taylorized regime are tough and where possible ruthless. All reward is based on carrot and stick principles, piecework is implemented wherever possible. Blame culture is at its worst, and this works in all directions.

Once Taylorism has taken a hold it becomes almost impossible to eradicate and can only be done by a strong-willed, powerful and visionary chief executive. Taylorism is self-sustaining because no one dares risk change. Managers in a Taylorist regime, however much they may dislike the system, will be aware that they have personally progressed despite the system. They may wonder whether they would survive if the rules of the game were to change. Having spent their lives achieving their current position, it will take considerable courage to try something new.

The Taylor-style management will also be wary of schemes that empower the worker. After years of indoctrination in an open warfare world, some will feel that they are handing their rifle to the enemy. This is strong stuff, and it is doubtful whether the organization exists which quite fits this hostile description, but some element exists at all levels in most organizations under the influence of Taylorism. Most people are fearful of change, fearful of the unknown. Usually, to change anything in any scale requires a shock, or alternatively a great deal of time. Time is the one thing western organizations do not have, so shock might be the only way. People confronted with shock will react, and the only way to ensure that the reaction is in the intended direction is through education. If change does not take place and quickly, there may be no future. In times of recession, businesses make drastic changes, sometimes too late, because they are shocked into doing so. In many cases they probably knew they were inefficient long before disaster struck, but procrastinated because they could not face up to the challenges. Some businesses have gone under because the directors could not bring themselves to make the necessary changes even when there was no alternative.

One chief executive shocked his managers into acceptance of change in the following way. He said: 'We have hired a consultant to talk to you all about participation and afterwards we are going to do it.' Sometimes theory 'x' is required to achieve theory 'y'. He knew that one simple statement like that was not enough. He had no doubt whatsoever. Afterwards, as the changes were introduced, he never took his eyes off the managers for an instant and, like it or not, eventually everyone of them became supportive. This all began in 1982. Now, it has become the way the company manages its people. The success of the Quality Circles is dependent more on the support of the managers than on the direct employees. Virtually all of the failures in Quality Control Circle programmes have been caused by lack of management support, or even in many cases, open opposition. Persuasion also works, but it takes longer and time is not on most companies' side. The resolute managing director with a clear vision of running an organization in which everyone participates has no substitute, provided of course that he stays long enough to see things through.

Strategy for the chief executive

The achievement of an organization in which everyone participates is no mean achievement, but the reward is worth the effort. Basically, the object should be to build an organization in which everyone from the top to the bottom is involved in working towards making their organization the best. Any organization which achieves this goal will always win against one which has not and where departments compete with departments, workers are against management, etc. Figure 6.7 illustrates the theory.

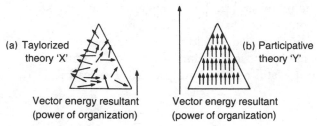

(a) Taylorized theory 'X'

Vector energy resultant
(power of organization)

(b) Participative theory 'Y'

Vector energy resultant
(power of organization)

Figure 6.7   Participative vs Taylorized organization

The power of an organization is the sum total of all the positive effort less the effect of negative effort. Internal conflict is negative and harmful to everyone in the organization. Positive energy at the bottom will be negated by resistance from the middle. Positive energy in the middle will be negated by resistance from the top. However, if the top is positive then positive energy from the middle will flow through. The same action applies between the middle and bottom. It follows that an organization can only be positive if the top is also positive. Therefore, the top must become positive first and this must begin with the chief executive. Quality Control Circle programmes have failed mainly because of negative attitudes either in the middle or top.

Rule 1   If the chairman and managing director remain unconvinced about Total Quality, forget it until they have been converted or replaced.

Rule 2   The chairman and managing director must convince the other directors. If they remain unconvinced, question their judgement!

Rule 3   Only when the Board is convinced, begin to seek converts at senior level. It is not necessary to convince everyone simultaneously. It probably isn't even possible. The results achieved by those who are supportive should convince the others. If not, question their suitability. Remember, some will appear unconvinced because they have been fooled before. How long is it until the MD retires or moves on?

Rule 4   Seek converts in lower echelons of the organization, primarily in the departments headed by supporters.

Rule 5   Take this procedure right through to direct supervision along the above principles.

Rule 6   Begin cross-functional teamwork activities among managers and specialists in supportive departments.

Rule 7   Involve other departments as soon as support is obtained.

Rule 8   Introduce the concept of Quality Control Circles to the workforce, the union and to line management and the specialists.

Rule 9   Commence Quality Control Circle activities.

Rule 10   Education and development is an ongoing activity. Improvement is always possible. Start suggestion schemes.

Rule 11   If it is still not working properly, re-read Rule 1.

7 Systems, ISO 9000 and BS 5750 in context

This chapter covers all aspects of ISO 9000 and BS 5750 – and why Japanese Total Quality organizations have not adopted these standards – to great effect! In particular, it discusses:

- Supplier evaluation
- The problems of third party assessment
- The benefits of single sourcing
- The role of national and international quality awards as benchmarks for success

Supplier evaluation

High quality demands professionalism in all activities and at all levels. Professionalism cannot be achieved through sloppy methods, vague instructions and unclear or non-existent policies or procedures. The history of most organizations, even those that are professional, indicates that they sometimes run into trouble because something was done in an unauthorized way, or because a modified procedure had not been put into effect. Many large organizations are professional and in the main have reasonably well-organized systems, but not all. Further down the line from medium-sized companies to the very small, the likelihood is that systems are less well defined, and concomitant problems become more common. That is why the need for some kind of organized approach to defining good systems and procedures was developed. Today's approach is through standards such as the ISO 9000 series and its national equivalents, i.e. BS 5750 series in the United Kingdom, the EN 29000 series in the European Community, and so forth.

Since 1982 the British Government has supported a national drive towards better quality, based on the promotion of these standards. The campaign has been extremely successful, and BS 5750 has now penetrated almost all sectors of business – manufacturing, processing, retailing, banks, building societies, local authorities and even the medical profession, including dental practices, and the legal profession. However, it is the opinion of the author that too much emphasis has been placed on the results achievable through the application of these standards to the extent that insufficient attention has been given to other quality-related concepts that are at least as important.

The need for organizations to sharpen up in these areas is undeniable, and it is not difficult to see how many quality calamities could have been avoided if schemes like this had been in place and operational before disaster struck. For example, in the case of the Zeebrugge ferry disaster, the crew member responsible for closing the bow door was apparently not at his station at the time of departure and consequently the door was not closed. Much of the debate in the case that followed centred on the captain's responsibility. It is not the place here to comment on who was responsible, and the evidence has not been studied in any detail by the author, but the fact is that the captain did not know, and could not have known, whether the door was open or shut since there was no means of communication between the door and the bridge, and apparently the door was not visible from the captain's position.

If the ship had been audited to BS 5750 and if the closing of the door was important to safety, which it obviously was, then according to BS 5750 there should have been a clear, written procedure authorized by the captain. There should also have been a system whereby it was possible for the person responsible to check whether the procedure had or had not been carried out. There would also have been a clear internal audit procedure to ensure that all aspects of the procedures were carried out, that proper training had been given, that checks were conducted to ensure that the mechanism was in working order, and that such checks had been carried out.

There have been many occasions in manufacturing engineering when large numbers of wrong parts have been produced because someone used the wrong issue of a drawing or specification. Products have failed because authorized design procedures have not been carried out. Temporary staff have used equipment incorrectly because procedures well known to permanent staff had not been written down. Food manufacturers have been known to scrap vast quantities of food because the wrong ingredients have been added when the only employee who knew what to do was absent. The replacement employees just guessed!

It is clear that quality cannot be achieved without adequate systems and procedures. There can be no other argument, yet curiously, BS 5750 is not universally popular and often not with many of the companies that have implemented it. The reasons are not hard to find. Reactions to BS 5750 depend very much on why the organizations in question have confronted themselves with the issue of implementation.

Almost invariably, those who have adopted a positive view of BS 5750 or ISO 9000 include those who have looked at the standard and made a conscious decision to review their organization against the standard and then remedy the deficiencies before going for assessment, on the basis that the requirements make sense and that professionalism in organization is regarded as important. Equally, those who adopt a more negative attitude primarily include those who are forced to adopt the standard by their principal customers, or because their competitors have done so and they are afraid that they will lose market share if they don't follow suit. In such cases the organization will proceed towards BS 5750/ISO 9000 with extreme reluctance if not hostility. In most cases upper management will attempt to delegate as much as it can to lower levels of the organization to minimize any disruption to their own activities. The lack of enthusiasm will be apparent to everyone and the actions taken will be the minimum possible to achieve accreditation. In reality, the organization will operate two systems: one which they show the auditor, the other the way things really happen. Such a situation can only breed cynicism and a generally negative attitude towards quality. As time goes by, these attitudes will harden further because it will be readily observed that the organization is accumulating considerable costs to service its almost totally ineffective quality system and virtually none of the benefit. In most cases, the directors will not perceive and will certainly not admit that the fault may lie with them. To the people on the factory floor, quality will be seen as a policing activity. The Quality Department will be seen as a sop to the customer, will be blamed for everything, and unless the besieged quality manager has developed a rhinoceros' hide he or she will probably not survive for long. Those who have not experienced a situation like this may regard this scenario as a gross over-exaggeration. However, it is unfortunately experienced by the majority of companies that have been exposed to quality drives, where the main focus has been BS 5750 or ISO 9000.

In fact, the problem is even worse, catastrophically worse. It is a considerable misfortune that many of the principal advocates of systems-driven quality programmes both believe and argue that BS 5750/ISO 9000 is at the heart of Total Quality, and much of the official literature designed to encourage industry to adopt the standards deliberately sets out to give this impression. The literature raises expectations of improvements to profitability and cost reduction through the application of BS 5750/ISO 9000 to very high levels. Most of these materials highlight chief executives who declare that this has been their experience. Perhaps for them it is true. But it will not be true for the majority. What the advocates are doing is generalizing from special cases. For some companies there is no question that, before doing anything else, the systems and procedures should be properly established. In many such cases, there will be a perceived and real reduction in costs, particularly where quality-related costs are incurred as a result of such deficiencies. This will not be the case for all organizations. In some it may be right to begin with the introduction of statistical process control or a project by project programme where specific high cost or high capital-absorbing opportunities exist, for example, high inventory. The important thing is to adopt the approach that produces the highest potential gains in the shortest time. Then, when the positive benefits have been realized, extend the programme into other areas.

Third party assessment and supplier evaluation

Organizations whose quality depends to some degree on the quality performance of their suppliers must have some form of supplier evaluation. BS 5750/ISO 9000 originated from this need and is used in many cases by purchasing organizations as a basis for supplier selection. This is unfortunate and is already leading to disillusionment on the part of many purchasing bodies, particularly those outside the United Kingdom who purchase from the United Kingdom and elsewhere as yet unacquainted with the standards. Such bodies have often observed that the suppliers who have achieved BS 5750/ISO 9000 are no better, and are frequently worse, than the suppliers who do not have the standard. There is a very good reason for this. BS 5750/ISO 9000 was designed to evaluate the systems of an organization. There is nothing in BS 5750/ISO 9000 which ensures that:

1. Processes are adequate (they may be in control, but not necessarily adequate).

2. Management involvement takes place.
3. Improvement activities such as project teams and Quality Control Circles are active or effective.
4. Just in Time activities exist.
5. Statistical process control is properly understood and practised (it is mentioned).
6. Anything more than lip-service is paid to calibration and maintenance of measurement systems (they are mentioned).
7. Policy management takes place (beyond the scope of the standard). Theoretically, a company can make icecream in a bucket and achieve BS 5750/ISO 9000, whereas the most modern plant in Europe may not. There are many quality-related issues that go far beyond the scope of these standards.

A second and major flaw in the BS 5750/ISO 9000 concept is the principle of third party assessment. Prior to the existence of BS 5750/ISO 9000 an organization had little alternative but to conduct its own supplier evaluation. This could be done in two ways: (1) by supplier audit; (2) by supplier or vendor rating. These are not mutually exclusive and most professional organizations do both. Under the BS 5750/ISO 9000 regime assessment is conducted by one of a number of accreditation bodies. There are more than twenty such bodies in the United Kingdom and others in most of the various countries around the world. The two main bodies in the United Kingdom are the British Standards Institute and Lloyds. Since the introduction of these standards in the early 1980s, the tendency has been for companies gradually to withdraw from first party assessment and rely on the third party assessment results of the accreditation bodies. From the point of view of such bodies, this has been a remarkable success and it is likely that the trend has long since passed the point where it could be reversed. There is every chance that industry will live to regret this fact, and it is likely that, even today, its most serious implications are already well in evidence. Third party accreditation has probably cost the United Kingdom ten years of leadership in quality.

Third party assessment is not common in the United States and its application in Europe is patchy though increasing as a result of the publication of ISO 9000 and its EC equivalent, EN 29000. In both cases, there is more reliance on first and second party assessment than in the United Kingdom.

The well-known example of a major first party scheme is the

Ford Motor Company QI scheme. Under this scheme suppliers must satisfy criteria in line with ISO 9000 and there is a heavy emphasis on process control and managerial responsibility. Other leading companies such as Electrolux, Boeing, etc., operate their own schemes.

However, not only in the United States but also elsewhere in the world many companies are becoming increasingly concerned that they may not be able to export into Europe in the future if they fail to comply with ISO 9000. Consequently, there is a considerable thirst for knowledge in those places and many companies are applying for ISO 9000 registration whether they believe in it or not. This applies also to the Japanese.

A purchasing organization cannot simply abdicate from its responsibility of evaluating and rating its own suppliers.

A third party assessor cannot evaluate an organization in a way that gives confidence that that organization's products and services, deliveries, innovations and responsiveness to new demands will satisfy the specific requirements of its individual customers.

What happens when all a customer's suppliers have BS 5750/ISO 9000 and the differences that existed between them before BS 5750 remain evident? They will be forced to return to first party, or second party by trade organizations (on behalf of the purchaser), assessment, but the skills and core competencies of this complex activity will have long since been disbanded. It would take several years to develop such an approval to the point where it became effective. As stated earlier, BS 5750/ISO 9000 looks at systems, it does not look at processes, process control, skills evaluation (it mentions training) and the other essentials. These items may satisfy the third party auditor but can be regarded as totally inadequate if viewed by the first party organization. Also, it would be impossible for a third party auditing organization to employ staff with detailed knowledge of complex processes to conduct such assessments. The auditor may be required to audit a company producing video recording heads one day, a microchip manufacturer the next and a chemical plant the next. Is it likely that the same person will be able to evaluate the efficiency of a catalytic converter as one who can determine the means by which oxide layers are being deposited on microchips or the adjustment of graphite electrodes in steel making?

The Japanese do not use BS 5750/ISO 9000. Suppliers to leading Japanese organizations such as Toyota, Nissan, etc., have commented that when they first tendered for contracts with these organizations the customers did not recognize standards. What they did discover is that the Japanese are more interested in the past performance of the supplier and its ability to produce quality products consistently. This might require the supplier having good systems, but the Japanese think that it is the supplier's responsibility to determine how they get there. A second but perhaps equally important consideration for a potential Japanese purchasing body is the attitude and style of the company chairman. They believe that if this person inspires confidence in them, then the company's performance will be satisfactory. The principle of a single sourcing, long-term cooperative relationship, which develops between Japanese purchasing organizations and their suppliers, renders BS 5750/ISO 9000-type third party assessment obsolete. Toyota (and other Japanese companies) work so closely with the supplier on product design, process improvement, skills development, education and training, that there could be no application for third party assessment. Toyota's suppliers and distributors and dealers are respectively referred to as the 'Toyota Family'.

It is now well known that the Japanese prefer single sourcing of suppliers, i.e collaborative relationships. The supplier almost becomes part of the company. In the West the tendency has been towards multiple-sourced, competitive relationships, with the two would-be partners at arm's length. Unfortunately, the third party assessment approach encourages this type of relationship. There is considerable evidence that many organizations which are ignorant of the principles of quality are selecting suppliers on nothing other than the basis that they are listed as being accredited. This is an abdication of responsibility. The fact that these suppliers have indicated that they have done something is laudable, but it means nothing compared with what is necessary for the purchaser to be operating a truly Total Quality-based professional organisation.

Summary

Third party assessment schemes based on BS 5750/ISO 9000 have achieved unstoppable momentum. They began in the United Kingdom, spread to Continental Europe and are now spreading around the world. They are fed by three major components:

1. The unchallengeable logic of the standard itself.
2. The unfortunate tendency of company directors and senior

executives to delegate everything, even to those who have no direct connection with the organization itself. To them the concept of third party assessment is attractive. It relieves them of a major responsibility, particularly when they have been led to believe in the credibility of the approach. It is one of the worst examples of delegation equals abdication.

3.   Recognition by governments and the respected institutions.

The process can be expected to run for a further ten years, into the early decades of the twenty-first century. Meanwhile, the gap between Japan and the rest of the world will continue to widen, unless the process is stopped by Deming and Baldrige-type strategies as described below.

Eventually, those industries that manage to survive and the governments of countries whose industries have been taken down this blind alley will live to regret that they did not think all this through before it was too late.

Alternative strategies

One of the advantages of BS 5750/ISO 9000 is that at least within the scope of its clauses, it does provide some guidance to an organization on what should be done to improve its systems. In this respect, the document has value. The facility that the standard offers to enable systems auditing is probably beyond criticism. When used as an audit element within one's own organization, and when conducting first party audits of suppliers, with staff trained in the principles of audit and with lead assessor skills, a major element of Total Quality will have been achieved.

However, BS 5750/ISO 9000 looks positively pedestrian when compared with both the Japanese Deming Award criteria, the American Baldrige Award and the Quality Health Check (see Appendix I and III). In the case of the Baldrige Award a range of criteria are grouped into ten categories which together accrue a maximum of 1,000 points. The criteria of ISO 9000 would at best amount to approximately 300 points in the Baldrige scheme, but the difference doesn't end there. The Baldrige Award is competitive, with only two possible winners in each of three categories (this is currently under review) and requires both a written and oral examination to be taken by the chairman, managing director and directors of the business. This forms the basis of an in-depth examination of personnel

Table 7.1. The key similarities and differences between the Baldrige and Deming Awards

Similarities	Differences
Oral and written examination of directors	Baldrige Award is competitive
1,000-point rating	Deming Award non-competitive
Cover all levels and activities	Deming Award more emphasis on data gathering based on facts – use of statistical approach
General structure similar	Deming Award more emphasis on Quality Control Circle activities
	Baldrige Award – more emphasis on customer information
	Deming Award open to oversees companies

throughout the organization, partly against the established criteria of the Award and partly to check the statements of the directors.

The key similarities and differences between the Baldrige and Deming Awards are given in Table 7.1.

While the Deming Award is non-competitive, it is extremely difficult to achieve, and probably no more companies achieve it in one year than the competitive Baldrige Award in the United States. Since its inception in 1950, only about 120 companies have achieved this status. However, the awareness requirements have provided a target for Japanese industry and have certainly had a major influence on the approach of Japanese companies. This is confirmed by the fact that many companies, including those presented as case studies in this book, won the Deming Award only three or so years after they officially commenced Total Quality activity. One can be sure that the status of their quality-related activities were already at a high level before the formal introduction of Total Quality.

While the Baldrige Award has been introduced in the United States, only recently it is already evident that it is beginning to make a similar impact to the Deming Award. Thousands of companies each year apply for the Baldrige guidelines (which vary slightly from year to year), but very few actually apply to be evaluated.

At the time of writing it seems that a European award will soon be introduced along the lines of the Deming and Baldrige Awards criteria. Hopefully it will merge both sets of criteria because while there are strong similarities between the award requirements, they are differently focused and it would be possible to meet the requirements of Deming but fail Baldrige, and vice versa.

The self-auditing Total Quality health check (Appendix III, p. 188) takes account of the criteria of both awards and gives a guide on where the emphasis should be for a company Total Quality launch.

8 The problem-solving process

Problem-solving by project is the focus of this chapter. It covers:

- Continuous incremental improvement
- Project ownership
- Project identification
- Project selection
- Project description
- Project by project improvement
- Holding the gains

A project by project improvement process is central to the concept of Total Quality. Without it, Total Quality could not exist. Incremental improvement, day by day, committedly carried out by all levels makes Total Quality an unstoppable force. Of course, all businesses improve on an evolutionary scale. People learn new techniques and apply them, new technology becomes available, lessons are learned from competitors, third party research and development, benchmarking, and so on. This is an underlying effect available to all organizations. The need for survival forces at least some attention on the issue of improvement. What is more important is the rate of improvement. Dr Juran identified the phenomenon in the mid-1970s when he was reviewing the effect of Japanese competition on the American automobile industry. He observed that in 1950 the Japanese automotive industry was markedly inferior to that of the United States. In 1950, it took nearly ten times as many Japanese workers to build a car as were required by Ford. Today, the situation is reversed, but Ford haven't stood still. They are much better than they were and are continuing to improve. What has happened is that the Japanese have improved faster. Dr Juran postulated that the Japanese began to pass the American industry in around 1976 (see Figure 8.1).

It can be seen that the American industry continued to improve, but at an evolutionary rate. The Japanese motor industry improved

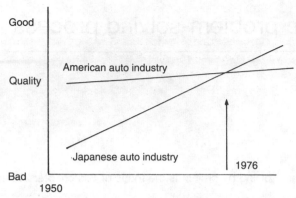

Figure 8.1   Improvement in Japanese vs US auto industry (Source: Dr J.M. Juran)

at a revolutionary rate, and so year after year the gap narrowed until it closed. If the two curves are examined more closely it can be seen that they are not a smooth line (Figure 8.1).

In the case of evolutionary improvement, the improvements are haphazard and unpredictable (see Figure 8.2). Figure 8.3 shows in detail the Japanese equivalent. Note that in the early stages, the increments were larger and more spaced. This is because in the 1950s the project by project improvement process introduced in 1954 by Dr Juran was entirely management-led with no worker involvement due to Taylor-style management. Then, in about 1962–5, the auto

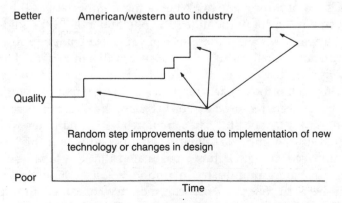

Figure 8.2   Evolutionary improvement in an organization

companies began to extend the improvement process down to the workforce. This resulted in more but smaller projects. Since these were in addition to management-led projects rather than instead of them, the effect was to increase the slope of the line. Later on, when the suggestion scheme process was also implemented, the slope increased again. In Japan, the key aim is to maximize the rate of increase on the slope. The greater the number of projects, the steeper the slope. Hundreds of projects mean hundreds of improvements. Of course, superimposed on top of all this will be the evolutionary improvements which are available to their competitors alike. All of the step improvements shown on the American/western industry curve are also available to the Japanese – such features as robot welding using microchips, machining centres. None of these items provides a competitive advantage because they are available to all. The competitive advantage comes from using existing technology more effectively than the competition. Interestingly, the use of high-tech operations does not always produce the expected benefits anyway. Much to the surprise of western observers on their first visit to Japan, they often find less automation than they expect, and in many cases far less than in their western equivalents. The Japanese believe that if an inefficient plant is automated its performance will worsen because the effect of the problems will be magnified.

The Japanese have calculated that the use of well-trained and efficient human labour is better than automatic assembly on several counts, for example, humans can walk to the work, whereas work

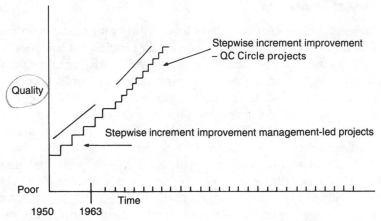

Figure 8.3 Stepwise improvement in a Total Quality organization

has to be taken to a machine. This is often forgotten in calculations for investment appraisal. A machine is usually dedicated to a single task and requires extensive reprogramming to do something different. A human is far more adaptable and more easily employed. A machine waiting for work can be an expensive commodity. A broken-down machine may cost more to fix than a sick worker. A person can provide subjective information and respond more readily to changes, and can make a wider variety of decisions. Of course, if people are used like robots, which is often the case in the West, then the advantages over machines quickly disappear. A human trained like a robot can answer back and go on strike. The answer is either to treat them like human beings and utilize their infinite capabilities or else buy a robot. But a word of warning. Robots become obsolete and, in any case, require maintenance by humans, and they will be the same kind of humans whose jobs the robots replaced because all humans have the same basic needs. Maybe it is better to learn how to treat people and find applications for the robots which no one wants to perform or which are too dangerous for people to perform.

Recognition of the power of project by project improvement in Japan has led to considerable focus on the means by which problems may be tackled. For the last two decades, the problem-solving team approach in Japan has become extremely sophisticated but the structure originally identified by Dr Juran can still be clearly seen.

Project ownership

Projects can be selected at any level within an organization from the Board of Directors through to direct and indirect employees.

Projects identified at higher levels within an organization can be tackled by those at that level or delegated downwards as appropriate. Projects identified from the middle may be tackled at that level or alternatively delegated downwards or recommended upwards depending upon the nature of the problem. Projects identified at the bottom in Quality Control Circle activities may either be tackled by them or recommended upwards. It can be seen that people at the top or middle of an organization will become involved not only in identifying, tackling and advocating projects themselves, but also in screening nominations from others. All this implies the need for some form of structure. This will be discussed in the next chapter.

Project identification

Brainstorming is the most popular and effective means by which projects are identified, although this method is by no means exclusive. One major food manufacturer found it necessary to conduct a major product recall because someone had found a small bone in one of its products. A project team was immediately set up to look into the causes of the problem and to find a remedy. Emergencies such as this tend to set their own priorities.

The object of brainstorming is to identify as many potential projects as possible; the technique can be used at all levels. When carried out correctly, brainstorming can be a remarkably penetrating technique, and ideas are usually put forward at a rate of around 70–100 in one period. If fewer ideas than this are put forward it is more likely that the brainstorming was not being taken seriously or the procedure not effective, than that there were fewer ideas. Usually, the ideas flow as fast as the person on the flip-chart is able to write. Using this approach, over 24,000 potential projects were identified at Short Bros by teams throughout the company. This is not unusual; it does not imply that the company is less efficient than any other. It does not matter how good an organization may be, there will always be a myriad of things which can be improved. Even with the world class performance of Toyota, which can be benchmarked against any company in any industry, over 2,600,000 improvements a year are proposed, of which over 96 per cent are implemented. It is interesting that the number topped the 2,000,000 mark in 1980 for the first time and then continued to rise. This does not indicate that Toyota are experiencing more problems, it means that even after three decades of the development of project by project improvement they are still improving their ability to find and tackle problems.

At Matsuchita one of the workers made an average of ten improvement suggestions a day! At Fuji Electric's vending machine plant, the workers make an average of ten suggestions per month per employee. Someone once said: 'We don't have problems, we only have opportunities.' This is exactly the case with problems identified in brainstorming. If the business is surviving today even with the burden of the problems identified, then with each problem tackled and solved the burden becomes lighter and performance improved. The ideas on a brainstorming list really are opportunities. Without them progress would indeed be difficult.

Brainstorming is one case where quantity is more important than quality. Provided that the quantity is there, the quality will be in the list somewhere. The next step is to sort the wheat from the chaff. The list will contain three types of problem: (1) those that can be tackled by the team itself; (2) those that are only partially within the scope of the team; and (3) those totally outside the scope of the team.

Problems only partially within the scope may require a specialist to join the group to give expert advice. In one company, which manufactured a famous brand of food blender, a team of workers in the gear blanking section found a project they wanted to tackle, but were aware that some of the problems required the assistance of a metallurgist. Since the company did not employ such a person, they hired the services of an expert from a local university. He attended a meeting with the group, became interested in the project and agreed to attend each of their meetings through to completion. The project was a great success and resulted in impressive savings.

Problems outside the group's scope can be passed to others if an organization structure exists for this to happen. This will be discussed in the next chapter.

Project selection

Projects chosen by a team should be selected from either the group initially classified as being 'totally group solvable' or from the partially solvable group, if the missing expertise has been made available. Incidentally, this may be personnel from other departments or occasionally another team which may have experience of other aspects of the project. Much benefit can be obtained from the development of the spirit of teamwork when two groups agree to work together.

The list of totally solvable projects will often include 20–40 nominations and (sometimes more), so further sorting will be necessary. In the early stages of the development of project by project improvement it is not advisable for newly formed groups to tackle problems which may be too difficult or take too long to solve. As a general rule, projects of about three months' duration with meetings of about two hours a week for management projects and thirty minutes to one hour a week for Quality Control Circles should be the target. This will normally narrow the list to some 3–10 potential projects. The final selection can include a range of criteria, including:

- Cost of the problem
- Availability of data

- Relevance to group
- Relevance to company goals
- Relevance to the department

Or any other criteria thought to be important

Project description

Project teams which have not been properly trained often run into difficulties because the project was not properly defined. This is an important consideration and can cause serious problems if it is reproduced throughout the whole Total Quality programme. There have been many cases where the whole structure has been put in jeopardy because all of the project teams have hit this problem simultaneously.

In Japan, this phase of a project is referred to as 'having a grasp of the current situation'. All members of the team must have a clear understanding of the nature of the problems and agree on the goals of the project. The most common cause of difficulties arises when the teams attempt to solve a 'solution' or a 'cause'. This may sound ridiculous but it is always happening when new groups are formed. The difficulty arises from the fact that in normal, everyday life, people rarely talk in terms of symptoms, which is what a problem really is. For the most part, people are sensitive to perceived needs. Consequently, when they brainstorm for the first time the result is a wish list, or a mixture of wishes and dogma related to causes, which infer blame or powerlessness. Examples of typical wish list items include:

Need a new computer
Need new or faster software
Larger car park ⎫
New plant ⎬ GROUP A
Bigger office
etc. ⎭

Examples of typical dogma include:

Lack of training
Poor communications ⎫
Lack of maintenance ⎬ GROUP B
The union
Poor supervision
etc. ⎭

All the items in Group A are remedies and all the items in Group B are 'causes'. The key question in both cases should be: 'Remedies to what?' and 'Causes of what?' Answers to both questions will lead to the problem, which the idea suggested in the brainstorming is believed either to remedy or be the cause of. It is only from this point that the problem can be solved. This seems obvious, but it is not, and the difficulty carries many problems for project teams. Experience indicates that it is worth spending some considerable time getting this right. It will make life very much easier later.

Problem-solving

There are two ways in which problems can be solved:

1. Go direct from symptom to remedy.
2. Go from symptom to cause to remedy.

Both are possible, but are not applicable to all problems. In industry generally, the tendency is to attempt to use method 1 all the time because route 2 is slower and requires organization. Unless a formal Total Quality structure exists the majority of problems which are present in organizations are there for no other reason than that there is no structured approach to tackle such problems.

For method 1 to be applicable it is necessary to be sufficiently familiar with the symptoms and the cause for the remedy to be fairly obvious. The likelihood is that the majority of such problems will already have been solved. Without formal problem-solving skills, problems can only be tackled by discussion. In some cases, this will also work, but again, in the majority of cases it will not. Most deep-seated problems cannot be solved by discussion or with opinion data. Perhaps they could be if everyone held the same opinion and it happened to be correct. More usually, the opinions conflict with each other and are based on unscientific and subjective data. Such data are notoriously unreliable, and are highly subjective.

Consider the following, very common scenario. A company produces a product, 'X'. Over the years the company has acquired an unenviable reputation for being late with its deliveries. From time to time, the problem becomes serious and some hard talking between the managers follows. The Operations Department manager will, in all probability, accuse the Maintenance Department of not repairing the equipment: 'If the equipment didn't break down so often, I would have met my schedule requirements.' Or 'If Maintenance attended to breakdowns more quickly . . . Or 'The Scheduling Department gave product "Y" procedence over "X" which lost several hours in making adjustments.' The Maintenance Department manager's response will be: 'If you looked after the equipment better, it wouldn't break down' and so it goes on.

All of these comments have some truth in them but are presented in an accusing, blame-oriented way, and no one has any intention of getting the facts together to prove them right or wrong. The person whose argument sounds convincing will win the day, but the problem will still be with them.

The only way to solve these sorts of problem is to do so scientifically, employing decisions based on facts. This requires a step-wise approach. The journey from symptom to cause has two key elements:

1. Identify theories of causes.
2. Test the theories to find the true cause.

Theories of causes can be suggested by anyone familiar with the problem. This includes technical specialists, line management, direct employees and other departments in the process chain.

Brainstorming can be used to identify theories of causes, but it is a fairly blunt instrument when used for this purpose. It would be better to employ process analysis or cause analysis if the problem is specific to an operation within a process. Both of these are brainstorming techniques, but instead of simply listing the ideas randomly, they are sorted as suggested and grouped with sub-causes and sub-sub-causes in order to highlight associations. The result of process analysis is shown in Figure 8.4.

Here it can be seen that one small problem, 'late deliveries', can be broken down into multiple sub-problems, which manifest themselves at various stages in the process. In a real situation the number of potential causes will be far greater than indicated here. If Design, Finance, Personnel, Maintenance and other related departments or functions had been added, an extremely complex picture would emerge. No wonder so many problems remain unsolved. Of course, not all of the sub-problems are of equal importance. The 80/20 principle will almost certainly apply here. That is, 80 per cent of the late deliveries will be caused by about 20 per cent of the items. The next step is to attempt to track them down. This is done through data collection and analysis. Since this can be time-consuming, people are often reluctant to take it on. What is more, the skill to do so may

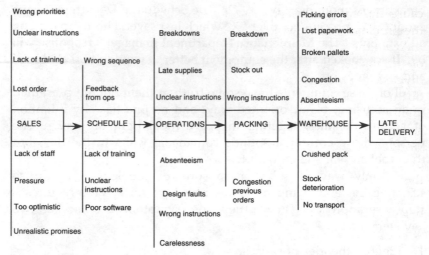

Figure 8.4   Process analysis to show associations in brainstorming

be lacking as well as lack of time. This is yet another manifestation of the problems outlined in Chapter 5. Before collecting data, much time can be saved by first looking for clues in the process analysis diagram. Notice the frequency of 'wrong or unclear instructions'! When a cause appears to repeat itself at different points it is an indication that there may be a chronic or inherent weakness in the organization. Once identified, checked and found to be the case, the pay-off will be that the solution to this problem will often, go someway towards solving other problems.

Simply looking for repeated causes is only one approach. Asking people who work in the area for their opinions is another. This, together with the hunches of the team members, will enable the selection of the most likely causes. Then the data can be analyzed and studied in greater depth. Consider again 'breakdowns' in operations. Data collection might reveal that a particular piece of equipment is more subject to breakdown than others. This then becomes a sub-problem of the overall problem and must be remedied if any major improvement to the real problem of late deliveries is to be achieved. Process analysis does not apply here because the team is looking at one specific activity. Instead, the team would probably use one of a number of techniques, e.g. tree diagrams, relationships diagrams, matrix diagrams or the cause classification diagram. Of these, the cause classification diagram is the most popular. Figure 8.5 shows the problem breakdown.

Again the problem 'breakdown' which is itself only a sub-element of the main problem ('late deliveries') has now been further sub-divided into thirteen sub-sub-causes. Some of these could be broken down further. When you consider that almost all of the problems identified in the process analysis can also be broken down in the same way, the whole thing begins to seem unmanageable. No wonder so many problems remain unsolved and cannot be solved by discussion. As this example shows, each of the sub-causes and the sub-sub-causes has its own remedies. They cannot be resolved by exhortation: 'From now on, let's have no more late deliveries' will be a totally ineffective demand. Without a structured and systematic approach using specially developed problem-solving tools, these problems will never go away. Nor will they disappear with the introduction of advanced technology. A new piece of plant may well be more reliable than its predecessor and less subject to breakdown, but it will still have problems of its own, and these will very quickly become apparent without the problem-solving process; they too will defy solution by discussion.

Having said that, dissemination of problem causes does have a pay-off – having broken the problem down in this way the remedies for each of the small elements are usually simple and often inexpensive. In reality there was no such thing as 'late deliveries'; that was merely the end-result of literally dozens of sub-causes, all

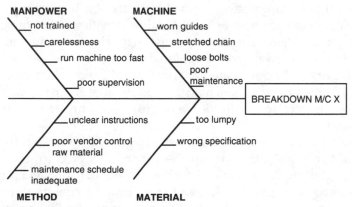

Figure 8.5 Cause classification diagram

of which must be addressed. Solving the problem of late deliveries is like trying to eat an elephant. First, it must be divided into bite-sized pieces. The process can be speeded up if others are asked to help. In the same way, a problem such as late deliveries can also be divided up and shared with project teams. Even Quality Control Circles may have a role to play.

Notice in the last example that the process analysis highlighted the sub-problem of lack of instructions, unclear instructions and lack of training. It is likely that a further examination of these sub-problems will indicate real weaknesses. The team will find remedies to these causes, apply the remedies and, if properly trained, foolproof the operation to ensure that there will be no recurrence. Systematically, project by project, over a period of time, virtually all systems-related problems will be addressed and resolved. They will have been resolved not by off-line Quality Assurance personnel, but by the workforce themselves. Quality for them will not be perceived as a policing activity but part of their own responsibilities. Quality through project by project improvement becomes part of everybody's job. Notice also that it is the responsibility of the organization in its attempts to be a world class company to choose to deal with these problems. BS 5750/ISO 9000 applied by coercion may give systems improvement a kick start, but without project by project improvement it is only a matter of time before such organizations regress to past practices.

Project by project improvement to overcome excessive order to delivery time

The company in question is small but part of a large group. At the time of commencement of Total Quality activities, the company had a major problem. The factory was relatively new and built on a greenfield site away from traditional industrial areas. Prior to that, the factory had been located in a traditional area, industrial relations had been poor and productivity so bad that the company was at risk in the marketplace, with its major customers threatening to cancel contracts.

The new plant was built with the target of £1.5 million turnover. Some two years after start-up the factory was producing only £1.2 million, but the floor area was congested with part-finished products. It seemed inconceivable that any more product could be produced. But one year later, the plant had a turnover of over £3.5 million, and the factory floor looked empty. This was a striking achievement. The product, a large steel cabinet packed with electrical components and complex wiring, had previously taken over three weeks to build, and defects were frequent. One year later the build-time had been reduced to four days, and defects were rare. Not only did the company cut its costs substantially, its profitability had increased considerably and the customers were sufficiently impressed that the company was awarded a larger share of the market. The improvement was not achieved by one single project, but through dozens of small projects mostly conducted by the workers in Quality Control Circle activities.

9 Implementing Total Quality

If you can dream it, you can make it happen.

Walt Disney

The chapter covers the practicalities of how to implement Total Quality. It discusses:

- Policy management, development and deployment
- Mission statements
- Critical success factors linked to the mission
- Benchmarking and goals
- The annual quality audit
- The role of the Quality Council

There is only one pre-requisite for starting Total Quality. The total commitment of the chief executive. The Deming and Baldrige Awards both demand a written and oral examination of the chief executive and the Board of Directors before moving to the next level. Total Quality operates through policy management, and without it, Total Quality is like a ship without a rudder. It may go somewhere and it may be in the desired direction, but only by chance.

Policy management

Whether policy management is formally introduced either before, during or after the other elements of Total Quality have become established is not relevant to success or failure, but policy management is the mortar which holds the bricks together and gives the whole process direction.

Policy management has three elements:

1. Policy development and goal-setting.
2. Goals deployment or dissemination
3. Policy control

Policy development

Since Total Quality is synonymous with the direction of the business and cannot be separated from it, Total Quality goals become the same as business goals. If the business goals are clear, then the techniques of Total Quality are deployed to enable these goals to be achieved. Frequently, the goals are not clear and so are not known or understood throughout the organization. Goals cannot be adequately set until there is agreement among the directors on the direction in which they want the business to go.

Typical goals for commercial organizations are growth, increased market share and improved profits. Since competing companies have similar ambitions, the achievement of these aims may not be easy. There will be both winners and losers. The winners will be those with the superior strategy *and* the means to achieve it. These two are not the same thing. An organization with a good strategy but poor performance will be at risk. Similarly, an organization with a poor strategy but good performance will be at risk. The aim must be to develop a superior strategy and deliver the best performance.

Strategy derives from vision. No person and no organization can succeed without vision. Vision stimulates the passion to succeed. Tom Peters, the author of *In Search of Excellence*, says that it doesn't matter which quality guru you follow, so long as you follow him passionately. The more the directors' and chairman's individual visions converge, the more likely will be the positive energy of the team. Remember the vector of energy (Figure 6.7). No two people will share the same vision by chance, and unless a conscious effort is made, it is unlikely that other people's visions will be known. Work must therefore be done to confide personal visions and work for their alignment. This can be a rewarding and fulfilling process, but is usually very hard work.

The articulation of the collective vision will be in the form of a mission statement. The mission statement is the most important vehicle for communicating the objectives of Total Quality to the organization and to external bodies as well. Mission statements usually contain an overall statement of the goals of the business, followed by a number of bullet lines on the means by which they will be achieved.

A typical mission statement will look like this:

> We are determined to make a product of such value and so attractive our customer will not only buy it, but recommend

it. Every single one of us can make an important contribution to accomplish this by finding and eliminating waste and continuously trying to improve the quality of what we do.

We will

- Provide the highest quality household refrigerator in the world, measured by
  - lowest service call rates
  - highest customer perceived value in fit, feel and finish
- Introduce product innovations to enhance our company's technological image with our customers
- Use state of the art manufacturing systems to
  - manufacture at lowest economical cost
  - provide optimum service to customers

This mission statement was created by the refrigerator division of Electrolux in the United States. What is important is the fact that it was developed by the top team collectively and it means something to them and they are proud of it. It gives them something to strive for, a sense of purpose. The fact that the company's vice-president and general manager was prepared to present a paper entitled 'The Mission Statement – a course of action and a means to measure' at a major international conference indicates the pride with which the statement was developed. In his paper, he said:

The development of our mission statement was not an easy exercise. It took several months to develop a statement that says what we intend to accomplish and how we will go about doing it. Many ideas were considered for inclusion in the mission statement such as profits, return on investment, market share, environmental issues, community responsibility, company environment, etc. All were eliminated after heated debate and we arrived at this simple focus that represents what we must do to be the quality leaders of the future.

Note the positive use of the word 'quality'. He went on to say that they had at the time of speaking trained 12 per cent of the hourly workforce in problem-solving techniques, and 50 per cent of the salaried workforce were trained in Juran-style task teams focused on management-assigned projects which impact directly on the customer.

Early results to date include: reduced supplier base from 235 in 1987 to 153 in 1988 with a target to reach 90 by 1990; ten vendors supplying materials on a JIT basis; dramatic improvements in the appearance of liners and doors; a 20 per cent reduction in scrap, resulting in an annual materials savings of over $8,000,000; finished goods inventory had been reduced from a 10–11-week supply to 6–7-week supply, with investment cut by almost $40,000,000; service call rates were reduced by 50 per cent over a three-year period.

There are many companies whose performance is such that one sometimes wonders whether their mission statements might look like this:

It is the policy of our company to produce the worst quality we can get away with, to charge as much as possible and to provide no service whatsoever. We will achieve this by:

1. Making our product impossible to service, while causing injury to the user whenever this is attempted.
2. Providing a customer information manual which is full of incomprehensible jargon that only the author can understand, but do it in such a way that the reader is made to feel inferior. Wherever possible translate the instructions from a foreign language, misspelling some words and not correcting the grammar.
3. Employees will be told nothing other than that required to perform their specific tasks. Accepting responsibility for deficiences will result in instant dismissal. Workers are not allowed to use the restaurant or the car park.
4. Any defects discovered will be blamed on the customer wherever possible, otherwise on suppliers, distributors or subcontractors as appropriate.
5. Designers are forbidden to communicate with market research or with production. They will concentrate only on designs which use the cheapest grades of material and use the minimum number of parts. It is the responsibility of marketing to devise ways to sell the products and for manufacturing to find the means to manufacture.

Critical success factors

The mission statement provides a focus for Total Quality and leads directly to the identification of key or critical success factors. The savings achieved above are typical of the achievements in a well-directed programme. Some of the savings are staggering. Critical success factor identification is essential if the full benefits of Total Quality are to be realized. An effective approach will be to select each bullet in the mission statement individually, and attempt to identify all of the specific performance criteria to which they relate. Goals or targets for each of these can then be agreed. Using the Electrolux example, note that service calls were reduced by approximately 50 per cent. This improvement was based on an Electrolux target of 50 per cent in 1989 and a further 50 per cent reduction in 1990. Achievement was very close to the goal.

Notice, too, that the goal was set incrementally over two years. The time horizon for major goals may be more or less than two years, and three years represents a reasonable period – the average length of service of the typical executive. Hopefully, this will change in the future.

Halving quality-related costs over a three-year period is a demanding assignment but is achievable. Ideally, critical success factors will comprise two elements: (1) internal goals: and (2) external goals targeted at the competition.

Internal goals are easy to understand. They include all of the inefficiencies within the organization, as well as such external factors as responsiveness to customer requirements, lead-time reduction, reduction in service calls, etc. External goals relate to competitive benchmarking and break down further into three sub-elements:

1. Customer perceptions of the organization compared with the competition.
2. Own perception of strengths and weaknesses against the competition.
3. Competitive benchmarking against the best in class criteria.

(1) is not the same as (2). For example, (2) will include features such as success in competitive bidding, competitors' cost to produce, prior franchise, and so forth. These will affect customers, but they will be more sensitive to factors that impact on them directly.

Customer perceptions

Collecting data on item (1) is important and appears to be a major weakness in western companies compared with Japanese. We saw in Chapters 3 and 4 the Japanese companies' high level of sensitivity to the importance of customer satisfaction and the role of market research.

Customer opinion surveys are an excellent way to collect data on customer satisfaction. Usually, when organizations do this for the first time, they receive some unpleasant feedback. In the absence of such data, organizations tend to rely on the subjective opinions of staff and customer complaints. The absence of complaints is no indicator of quality reputation, the false premise in this respect being that satisfaction is the opposite of dissatisfaction. Between these two extremes lies indifference, and this is the worst place of all because it gives no feedback. On the other hand, an extremely satisfied customer and an extremely dissatisfied customer are both likely to make their feelings known.

Peter Drucker, the leading American management consultant, once said that to be successful in business it is necessary to be better than the competitor at something. That was in the 1960s. Today that is no longer good enough. Now it is necessary to be best at as many things as possible. This requires market feedback. Komatsu have what they call 'green groups'. A green group is a team of customers and company personnel who meet regularly to discuss needs, trends and new product projections with the aim of supplying products and services which always satisfy the customer.

Strengths and weaknesses against competition

Strengths and weaknesses against competition lead to two opportunities with Total Quality.

Where a competitive weakness (or competitor strength) is identified an immediate opportunity exists to establish a challenging project. The competitive spirit is strong in organizations and it is better to have teams competing with the market competitor than with other parts of the organization. Japanese companies encourage the idea of the common enemy. Komatsu used the slogan 'Encircle Caterpillar'. One of the automotive manufacturers created the slogan 'Beat Benz'; another 'Beat Porsche'.

The strength can be exploited by sensitizing customers to raise their expectations in the direction of core competences of this organization and away from those of the competitor. Sometimes these may be irrelevant to the customer, but they will admire the effect and are likely to be influenced by it.

Benchmarking

Most of the activities in any organization are similar. Apart from the specific operations which identify the business of industry, most other activities are function-centred rather than industry-specific. For example, people in personnel can work in any industry, and individuals can and do move from banking to engineering, to hotels, the media, to the travel industry or anywhere. The same applies to finance, administration, market research, purchasing, etc.

For all of these activities, regardless of industry, there are norms or standards which apply, for example:

- Labour turnover.
- Order processing.
- Use of software.
- Data processing.
- Debtor and creditor control.
- Product launch, etc.

The tendency today is to go beyond competitor analysis and seek the best in class, irrespective of industry. It is predicted that benchmarking will become a hot topic in the next decade.

Figure 9.1 summarizes the aspect of policy management.

Annual goals

The three-year critical success factors comprise a synthesis of internal goals, customer and competitor-related goals, but three years is a long time to wait to evaluate success. Annual goals should be established to create relatively quick targets (see Figure 9.2).

Again, the customer service target of the Electrolux factory serves as an example. These goals should span all functions of the business

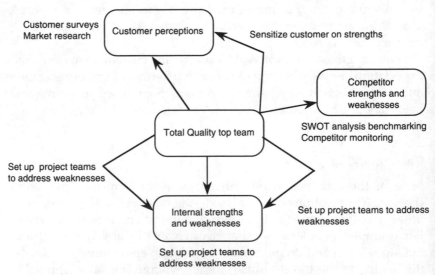

Figure 9.1 The use of project teams to address weaknesses

and be challenging but achievable. This completes the work of the company's top team in Total Quality development, but the scale of the task must not be underestimated. Many western companies will spend about three days a year on this exercise and these sessions are referred to as 'Back to the Woods'. A typical Japanese Board of Directors will spend six months doing nothing else. This is their prime responsibility. Note that in the Electrolux example the executive said that he and his colleagues had spent months refining the wording of the mission statement. This was a great deal of time, but look at the savings that resulted from this action. On the other hand, there are other organizations where the mission statement appears mysteriously out of the managing director's briefcase, the result of one or two hours' work the night before. It looks impressive, but is probably meaningless. No wonder no one is impressed.

Establishing the structure

Whether or not the top team chooses to go though the exercise outlined above before commencing Total Quality activities is optional and makes little difference to the overall success of the process. At some stage it will be necessary to set up project by project improvement teams. These take time to develop to the point where

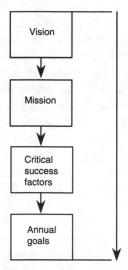

Figure 9.2   The work of the top team

they become effective, and the first projects they tackle should not be too difficult or too lengthy. It is therefore not important whether or not these projects relate to the annual goals established in policy management. In fact, it is probably better at this stage to allow the newly formed teams to identify their own projects, since the problems they tackle will be important to them, and they will gain satisfaction from the results.

If project team training takes place prior to or in parallel with the establishment of policy management, it means that at least a basic resource of project teams can be established to commence activities related to the goals as soon as these have been determined. In some organizations, policy management development has been deferred for as long as eighteen months from the date of start-up in order to get the project by project process established.

Facilitator and team leader training

Some companies favour the idea of full-time facilitators or project team support personnel. Others do this on a part-time basis. In the case of project teams as opposed to Quality Control Circles, again, the differences in performance between the two alternatives is undetectable. The result depends more on the personalities of the facilitators and the support they are given by the organization as a whole. If the organization is supportive, then facilitation is easy, whichever path is chosen. The only real drawback to part-time facilitation is the risk of a clash between the demands of the team and the facilitators' other responsibilities, but this does not usually become a major issue. One approach which is proving to have positive benefits is an extension of the part-time facilitator approach, where the facilitator of one team is the leader of another. The advantage here is that both facilitator and leader can appreciate the needs of the other. Also, because the individuals are outside the process offering guidance in the facilitating role, they have a better appreciation of their own situation when dealing with their own project. Also, it means that no one is spending too much time on facilitation. The method has much merit.

Policy deployment or dissemination

When the project process has been resourced with trained team leaders and trained facilitators, it becomes possible to deploy the goals down through the organization. This takes place layer by layer through to the lowest level.

Initially, the annual goals established in policy development will be disseminated to each of the division or department heads, at which point the goals are carefully analyzed. Some of these goals will not be relevant to every department, or if they are, it may be necessary to change the vocabulary. For example, a goal at director level called 'yield' may be interpreted as 'scrap reduction' in one department or 'downtime' in another. These restated goals will be agreed between the directors and the department. Following this, the goals go down yet another layer and again the process of reinterpretation is repeated. Eventually, the dissemination process will cascade to the base of the pyramid. However, at this stage Quality Control Circle activities will not have been started and so there will be a delay before the process is taken right through. Typically, it will take some three years to reach a point where everyone becomes involved in an average-sized company. Of course the actual rate will vary depending upon the resources devoted by the organization to implementation. Short Bros took the process through almost the whole organization in the first year as a result of a massive training programme. It is really just a matter of choice, depending on how much money is available and how soon the results are required. Figure 9.3 illustrates the deployment process.

Feedback loop

Once the deployment process is complete, work can begin at all levels of the organization. Some of the improvements will come through projects; the rest require working more effectively or come through individual suggestions. However, in a Total Quality organization this process is not left to chance. A feedback loop must be established at all levels from the bottom to the top. At the base of the pyramid, the feedback will be hourly and daily. At each subsequent layer the feedback will be in progressively longer cycles, through to branch or divisional heads' half-yearly returns. The feedback will contain two elements; feedback on projects and feedback on daily performance.

Annual audit and review

The top team, having set the whole process in motion, will obviously want to be sure that their investment has been well placed and will

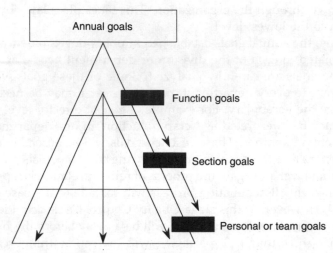

Figure 9.3 The deployment process

undoubtedly monitor results on a regular basis. In addition to this, a formal audit conducted by the chairman and managing director (in Japan, the president's audit) should be carried out at all levels. The audit has a double benefit. First, it will reveal the extent to which the Total Quality programme has been effective; secondly, but at least as important, the audit will demonstrate the commitment and depth of understanding of the company's top people.

The audit will inevitably reveal weaknesses and also, features where the results exceeded expectations. The review will help in the process of setting new goals for the following year and at the same time provide an opportunity to review long-term goals as well. The marketplace will probably have changed and this will affect the long-term, medium-term and annual goals. These are rolling targets and can be changed at any time, if the change results in a competitive advantage.

Recognition and reward

Total Quality can be implemented in two ways: either by using threats and fear (theory 'x'), or by making the work itself more enjoyable and rewarding (theory 'y'). Both methods work, but all the current evidence stacks in favour of the theory 'y' being far and away the more successful. Total Quality is in itself pure theory 'y'. If people are to get pleasure out of their work, then the work itself must fulfil personal needs. This might seem impossible for some tasks, but even for the most unpleasant work, a few simple ideas can make a significant difference:

- All people want recognition.
- All people want to be listened to.
- Everyone wants to think that their job is important.
- People like challenges.
- People like to develop and gain merit.

All of these needs can be satisfied through project by project improvement, Quality Control Circles and suggestion schemes if a structural approach to presentations of successful projects, publicity and some form of awards (which do not have to be financial) exists. All successful Total Quality companies do this and the obvious attractions of both the Deming and Baldrige Awards indicate that companies do too.

Quality Council

The Quality Council is the top team referred to above. Some companies like to give the top team some special identity when they are dealing with Total Quality issues; others do not. It does not really matter, but to use a label of some sort does have some advantages. First, it raises the profile of Total Quality and gives visibility to the Total Quality-related activities of the board or top team. Second, it separates the Total Quality issues from the day to day activities in running the business. Many may think this is a disadvantage because, after all, throughout this volume we have laboured the point that Total Quality is the process of running the business. This is true but, by introducing Total Quality for the first time, the business is intending to change from one state to another. The question then arises: 'How do we go from here to there?' (Figure 9.4). If all of the issues related to this change simply appear on a board meeting agenda lumped together under the heading Total Quality, then trouble will almost certainly ensue.

If Total Quality appears as item 8 on the agenda item 7 may take longer than it should and item 8 falls off the bottom. The issues are held over. This will bring about the downfall of the programme and this will be noted. At the next meeting, Total Quality will be even

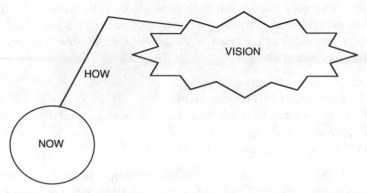

Figure 9.4 The relationship between Total Quality and management vision

more vulnerable and eventually it will fall off altogether. The end will be in sight.

The advantage of forming a Quality Council is that Total Quality will have its own agenda and its own issues. When Total Quality has become a way of life – and that could take several years – then Total Quality can be merged with the normal agenda. It will have become the way things get done. By that time, the business will probably be the top in the world anyway!

Finally, don't forget:

- Statistical process control
- Just in Time
- Total productive maintenance
- Suggestion schemes

There is much to do and no time to waste!

Total Quality represents a new way of life at work; the start of a new era in management and the beginning of a new industrial culture in which everybody wins; where pride, dignity, self-respect and mutual respect are the hallmarks of the truly Total Quality-driven organization.

Conclusion

By now it is likely that serious readers will have drawn the conclusion that there is nothing really new in Total Quality, and they would be right. Put in its simplest terms, Total Quality represents nothing more or less than the collective professionalism of everyone in an enterprise. All the individual concepts that form part of Total Quality have existed for decades, and in some cases possibly for centuries. What is different is the way in which all the concepts and techniques are pulled together into a mutually supportive framework, held together by some fundamental beliefs.

The essence of these beliefs is contained in Chapter 6, which challenges the western perception of managing people, and in Chapter 9, which describes the role of the top team. It is this group alone which determines the culture of the organization, and which decides strategy in the marketplace. Total Quality is totally dependent on the support and involvement of this most senior group. Top managers like to delegate, but this is a case where delegation equals abdication. However, culture is one thing, but without clear goals – and the means to achieve these goals – nothing will happen. Chapters 5, 6 and 7 focus on the key tools and techniques which have proved to be so successful in world class Total Quality companies. These techniques have all been used both within and without the Total Quality philosophy. On their own they prove unimpressive; within a Total Quality culture the results are exceptional.

Not only does Total Quality create winning organizations, it may also bring about the untimely demise of those organizations that fail to achieve its high standards. No longer can industry afford the luxury of deciding whether or not to adopt Total Quality. It is only a matter of when and how. I hope this book may have helped to stimulate action now!

Appendix I
A brief history of Total Quality

Its roots in Japan

The term Total Quality Control originated in the United States in the mid- to late 1950s. The first reference to the term appeared in an article by Dr A. V. Fiegenbaum (in *Harvard Business Review*, Vol. 34, No. 6, Nov–Dec. 1956, pp. 93–101), and again in his *Total Quality Control, Engineering and Management* (McGraw-Hill, 1961).

Total Quality today is markedly different from anything envisaged by its American pioneers. Total Quality Control, as perceived by its American gurus, had its origins in mass production and Taylorism. At that time, Taylor-style management was at its climax in the United States and unchallenged even by the behavioural scientists. Quality Control as a science has its roots in the origins of mass production, notably in the Ford Motor Company. Ford was the first pioneer of any significance to take Taylor's ideas on the division of labour and apply them to high-volume manufacture, with the introduction of the moving track.

Prior to its introduction by Henry Ford, vehicles were manufactured on a plinth, and the workers and components came to the vehicle. Under Ford's system, the part-assembled vehicle came to the worker and to the parts, which were stored alongside the moving track. This system effectively eliminated all vestiges of craftsmanship from the process. Work became so monotonous, tough and stressful that, not surprisingly, the worker could not be relied upon to demonstrate care in workmanship. Quality deficiencies in the form of missing parts, loose bolts, misalignments and damage became major problems.

The remedy was to create an army of off-line inspectors as a post-operation policing activity. This was the origin of western-style Quality Control. It soon became evident that post-operation inspection was unsatisfactory since it did nothing to prevent the occurrence of defects. It doesn't matter how much a defective part is inspected, it will not make it any better. All inspection can do is to segregate good from bad, and it is not particularly good at doing that. There have been many studies of high-volume inspection and it is evident that inspectors are highly fallible even to the point that in some situations they will miss over 90 per cent of defects. There is considerable evidence from research that the very fact that they are human ensures that they will miss at least 10 per cent, however obvious the defect may be. On the other hand, inspecting a good product only adds to its cost, not to its value.

The next step in the evolution of quality was how to prevent defects in the first place.

This was the birth of Quality Control, but it did not challenge the Taylor system which was creating the problem. Instead, the American Quality pioneers concentrated their efforts on reducing defect levels under the existing Taylor regime. The first breakthrough came when Dr Walter Shewhart, a statistician, was appointed to head the Quality Control activities at the Hawthorn Works of the Western Electric Corporation. This was a massive plant employing some 40,000 workers on relay assembly. On his staff was an up and coming engineer named Dr Juran, Dr Levenforth, of Grant & Levenforth fame, and Dr Elton Mayo. Dr Shewhart quickly recognized the opportunity for the application of his statistical background to the inspection function and invented the $\bar{X}/R$ chart concept (see p. 106). Interestingly, Dr Juran was the first person to use the technique when he applied it to the manufacture of relays.

Following World War II, Statistical Quality Control was regarded as the state of the art and applicable mainly to the high-volume manufacture of engineering products. This was the situation when Dr Deming (1950) followed by Dr Juran (1954) and Dr Fiegenbaum (1958) went to Japan. Each of these gurus sees quality differently, but each of them regarded quality as a management activity and at that time Taylor's theory that 'management manages and people do' remained unchallenged. After all, the United States was the most powerful country on earth, largely as a result of Taylor-style management combined with the mass production concept.

During the 1950s the Japanese were not in a position to challenge any of these concepts. The slogan in Japan was 'First of all copy the West', which very rapidly changed to 'Catch up with the West!' The economy was in ruins after World War II. Japanese industry was inefficient and totally uncompetitive when compared with the United States. Japanese managers and engineers flooded over to the

United States and the Americans showed them everything in a spirit of total openness. Why shouldn't they? They could not imagine the Japanese as an economic threat. In the complacent words of John Foster Dulles, the American Foreign Secretary, in a speech he made in Tokyo in 1950: 'You will never be able to compete with the United States in technology, but you do make very good handkerchiefs and pyjamas which would sell very well in the USA, why don't you export these?'

Had it not been for the American courage to face up to the facts of life in the mid-1980s and respond to the challenge of Japanese supremacy, the roles could easily have been reversed. It will be interesting to see over the next few years whether the United States can recover its dominant position. One thing is certain. If it does, it will do so using concepts which may have some of their roots in the United States, but which will have been invented and made by the Japanese. What is more, the Japanese have done so by challenging the validity of other American management concepts. To give credit to the Americans, they have been the first to recognize and accept this fact. It is curious that Europeans are taking longer to do so.

Japanese Total Quality Control

Dr Masao Kogure, Professor Emeritus, Tokyo Institute of Technology, suggests that the four main conditions which describe true Japanese Total Quality Control are:

1. To provide quality combined with the needs of the consumer – products, services, information or anything else that can be marketed – by always bearing in mind customer orientation and quality assurance.
2. To encourage all corporate personnel, from management down to the factory floor to maximize their efforts to realize the objective given in condition 1 under the effective leadership of the company's chief executive.
3. To develop and make the most of scientific and statistical methods, in order to ensure that quality control activities are conducted rationally and effectively.
4. To establish and operate administrative systems in which personal dignity and independence are respected so that quality control may be conducted efficiently and continuously.

(Initially, the Japanese preferred the term 'Company-wide Quality Control' (CWQC) to avoid confusion with American-style Total Quality Control based on Taylorism.)

The author believes that it was in about 1952 – before Dr Juran's 1954 lecture – that Total Quality Control began. An issue of the magazine *TQC*, which was first published in March 1950 in Japan, states that in 1950, when Dr Deming gave a lecture, the magazine published many articles related to what was called SQC (statistical quality control). There were several stories giving accounts of SQC activities applied to production process management indicating that SQC was already in operation.

When Dr Deming held his seminar under the theme 'Sampling for Market Research and Studies', mounting interest provided one of the approaches towards satisfying condition number 1.

In July 1954 Dr Juran went to Japan to give two courses for company presidents and ten day courses for managers and section heads in Tokyo and Osaka. Those for top management were attended by about 130 people and those for managers and section heads had turnouts of about 300. In the words of Dr Kogure, 'The courses had a new and powerful impact on Japanese corporations which had initiated TQC around 1952.'

The courses presented definitive answers to detailed questions posed by Japanese companies, which were then facing many and varied problems at a time when the framework of TQC was being established. Dr Juran's lectures included:

1. The nature of control
2. Division of the subject
3. Economics of quality
4. Specification of quality
5. Manufacturing planning for quality
6. Production Department quality problems
7. Origination for inspection
8. Measurement
9. Vendor inspection
10. Process inspection
11. Final inspection and testing
12. The staff quality functions
13. Defect prevention
14. Quality assurance
15. Training for quality

16.   Quality mindedness
17.   The role of statistical methods

In the lectures, Dr Juran introduced ways of conducting Quality Control activities, for example, analysis of degrees of importance using the Pareto chart, the distinction between sporadic and chronic forms of inferiority, the selection of control points and the tools required for problem-solving. Again in the words of Dr Kogure:

It was probably the first time that, apart from postgraduate education in Japan, this type of group discussion, as usually found in American seats of learning, was adopted in courses given outside corporate halls sponsored by professional organisations. After that, the method was adopted in JUSE's [Japanese Union of Scientists and Engineers] courses for Managers and Section Chiefs as organised by their M. Committee and today it has emerged as an important means of instruction, highly popular in the realm of management.

And in the words of Dr Juran:

I was also impressed by the training which was then under way for applying statistical tools as an aid to control quality. This training has received a major impetus from Dr Deming's 1951 lectures. Nevertheless, it was my conclusion that there existed an imbalance. There was an over-emphasis on the use of the statistical tools and under-emphasis on making managing for quality a part of the overall process of managing the business. Similarly, there was over-emphasis on control and under-emphasis on quality improvement. This state of imbalance came as no surprise to me, since at that time a similar state of imbalance existed in the Western countries.

In later years these same conclusions were confirmed by Professor Ishikawa, Dr Kondo, Mr Miyauchi and others. However, it is obvious that the Japanese listened to Dr Juran's advice as will be evident from his account of the situation in 1960:

I revisited Japan during November and December of 1960. The contrast with 1954 was astonishing. The country was undergoing a universal boom of construction and modernisation. Productivity and salaries were rising sharply. An atmosphere of industrial progress was all pervasive.

In the field of quality, activity was also intense, the training programmes conducted by companies and by JUSE had grown to massive proportions. The over-emphasis on statistical methods had declined. Training in managing for quality had been extended widely to middle and lower levels of management. Training of supervisors had expanded remarkably through courses offered on the national radio as well as through company and JUSE courses. The first TV courses had begun. Collectively all that training represented a very large investment in time and money. The Japanese were paying the price, and thereby were becoming the best trained people on earth with respect to managing for quality.

Following this, the Japanese made further extensions of their Quality activities, this time to involve the workforce. Again, Dr Juran was able to witness the effect with the result that at the European Organization for Quality Control Annual Conference in Stockholm in 1966, he said, 'The Japanese Quality Control Circles movement is a tremendous one which no one else seems able to emulate, the Japanese are headed for world quality leadership and will attain it in the next two decades, because no one else is moving at the same pace.' Again, in the words of Dr Juran, 'That prediction was not taken very seriously by Western managers.'

The 1990s

What of our own situation in the West? Is there quality awareness? Yes, just as there was in Japan in the early 1950s.

Is the West on the right track? Probably not yet. Just as with Japan in the early 1950s with its overemphasis on SQC, the risk is that in the West today there is probably an overemphasis on the role of Quality Standards and ISO 9000 through third party assessment. To become competitive again, the West must show a marked shift in the next few years towards quality improvement. And there must be much more investment in education and training and, like both Japan and Singapore, a government drive in the right direction.

Appendix II
The international scene

In January 1980, Christopher Lorenz commented on the management page of *The Financial Times*: 'Quality will become the key issue of the 1980s.' He deserves full marks for that. Quality has become the hot topic worldwide. Let there be no doubt. The only reason for this has been the phenomenal expansion of Japanese export capability resulting from a quality-led industrial revolution comparable only with the United Kingdom's in the mid-nineteenth century. Two very small countries by international standards, each like a bookend at either end of the Euro-Asian continental landmass. What are the similarities? In both cases, quality was a premium. Even today, there are many people in Britain who can remember the expression 'British and Best', 'Workshop of the World', and so on. Between the ascendancy of Britain and the more recent advent of Japanese economic might, we have, of course, witnessed the excellence of German, Scandinavian, Dutch, Swiss, French, Italian and other fine European products, as well as the superiority of American military products, with their related stunning performance in space exploration, matched only by the Soviets.

All of these achievements demand quality of the highest level, and standards that stretch human creativity and capability. These are exciting features and demonstrate the positive aspect of quality. Of course, there is the equal and opposite negative face: the face of poor quality. It is ugly, can be disastrous and forever poses a threat to human life, and possibly to civilization itself.

Chernobyl in the Ukraine, the Exxon Valdez fiasco in Alaska, Bhopal in India, Three Mile Island in the United States – these and others too many to mention go down in history to provide an ever-present reminder of what can happen when things go wrong. Were these disasters caused deliberately? No, of course not, but no one can deny there was a quality failure. If they were not deliberate and everyone was trying to do a good job, then the nature of the organization itself must have been responsible and not the individual. Disasters of the magnitude described here cut across national boundaries. Today as never before, the quality sciences and disciplines affect us all. The experience of the 1980s has indicated that we have learned this fact.

The triennial World Quality Congress, which took place in Brighton in 1984, attracted 1,000 people. When it was next held in Tokyo in 1987, it attracted around 2,000. In 1990 in San Francisco the same event attracted over 4,000. In each case the participants came from all around the world to share their ideas. Quality is now a truly international concept. As one American speaker said at the European Organization for Quality Control Conference in Moscow in 1987: 'Quality is a concept which has no passport.'

Quality in the United States

The principal organization to support the development of quality in the United States is the American Society for Quality Control (ASQC). The major influence which the United States has enjoyed around the world since World War II is reflected in the influence of this organization, which has an international 'chapter' with representatives from many foreign countries including the UK. ASQC hosted the World Quality Congress in 1990 in San Francisco which was run concurrently with its own annual convention. This convention takes place annually in different locations around the United States and always attracts a large national gathering with a significant and growing number of international participants. The organization offers many services, both centrally and through its regional chapters. Its range of publications is impressive, and includes a wide selection from many of the world's most accredited quality authors. It also encourages the development of the quality sciences through a number of highly sought-after awards such as the Shewhart prize, the Lancaster prize, and so forth. The systems approach to quality is highly developed in the United States largely due to the defence and aerospace industries, but interest in ISO 9000 has only recently been aroused among those who wish to export to Europe. The Baldrige Award is having a greater impact. Until the more recent advent of Japanese specialists and pioneers in the field of quality, the United States has provided most of the world's most illustrious quality gurus.

Dr Walter Shewhart, who invented statistical quality control in the 1920s, was followed by Dr Juran, who stands head and shoulders above all of his rivals for no other reason than the sheer volume of his creative ideas. These have continuously provided industry with ever more challenging concepts and methods, in an almost unbroken stream since the 1930s and 1940s and continues even to this day. Without Dr Juran, the universal breakthrough sequence which forms the basis of virtually all successful project team and Quality Circles disciplines may never have been discovered.

Dr Deming, who has so ably presented Dr Shewhart's concepts and expanded on the use of the statistical method, has probably contributed more than most to the development of decision-making based on facts rather than opinion. Of more recent origin, his now famous fourteen points present something of a challenge to even the most professional manager.

Dr Fiegenbaum, another pioneer who is believed to have coined the term 'Total Quality Control', is also a consultant, author and pioneer whose work has influenced quality on an international basis.

It is not surprising that with such eminent men, the world has looked to the United States over the past decades for the lead in the development of quality methodology. It therefore came as something of a surprise to most people when, in the late 1970s, this lead suddenly and so decisively switched to Japan. The effect on the quality profession and on industry in general in the United States was traumatic.

Through the late 1970s into the 1980s all the classic signs of shock were evident. At first disbelief, then confusion, followed by panic measures. First it was Quality Circles, then SPC, then JIT, etc. All of these experiments were looking for the quick fix, the Holy Grail, and most were disappointed because, without exception, all these concepts are only part of Total Quality, and without the infrastructure none will be effective. However, gradually the lessons were learned. Towards the end of the 1980s, the first tangible signs of an understanding of the way back were beginning to appear. The term 'Total Quality Management' began to be used. Much of this was – and still is – 'hype'. Americans have a well-deserved reputation for this, and often it is useful. However, it is not useful when it is used to mask the truth, and when this happens it only feeds scepticism. Soon the hype gave way to real, measurable signs of success. Total Quality Management as it is often regrettably referred to had at last been identified as a serious contender for re-establishing the reputation of US industries. I say regrettably, because in my opinion the word 'management' should never have been incorporated into this term.

In any organization, at least 30 per cent of the personnel would not regard themselves as 'management' and yet, in Total Quality, their participation is essential. I always refer to 'Total Quality' and never to Total Quality Management. I argue that Total Quality embraces Total Quality Management. It also embraces other things, such as the voluntary participation of the workforce.

The Malcolm Baldrige Award

Having established that the concept of Total Quality demonstrably works and furthermore that companies such as Caterpillar, Xerox, McDougall Douglas, Motorola and others were achieving very significant improvements, the question arose, 'What must we do not only to encourage industry to follow them but to do so wholeheartedly?' Noting the importance that the Japanese attach to the 'All Japan Quality Award' and the 'Deming Award', it was soon realized that a national award was important in the United States. The Malcolm Baldrige Award was subsequently created by Public Law 100–107, signed into law on 20 August 1987.

Malcolm Baldrige served as Secretary of State for Commerce from 1981 until his death in 1987. As he had been a member of the team that drew up the criteria for the award, it was decided to make the award in his name. Prior to 1990 there had not been a winner in the Service category and, in 1989, there was no winner in the Small Business category.

The stringency of the evaluation is likely to prove a success for the award. Anything that is hard to achieve is likely to gain high prestige. The award winners are expected to share their strategies and demonstrate that their approaches are transferable.

Experience to date indicates that the high scorers tend to have:

- Aggressive quality goals, benchmarks and response time drivers
- Use of all conceivable customer listening opportunities
- Quantitative orientation
- Major human resource investments. (It was claimed that much of this resource was to overcome shortcomings in the educational system – doubtless the United States is not alone in this respect!)

The lower scorers tend to have:

- Passive leadership.
- Reactive customer systems.

- Limited benchmarks.
- Plateaux – got better, then levelled off!
- Partial quality systems – some bits but not everything, i.e. SQC, JIT, etc.
- Lack of evaluation process

Quality in Japan

Quality in Japan is now so well documented that virtually any coverage would only be repetition of much that has gone before. Surprisingly though, there has been little discussion of the Deming Award, and given the exposure of the Baldrige Award, this is surely appropriate.

The Deming Award

There are various categories of the Deming Award: the Deming Award for Literature, the Deming Award for Large Companies, for Small Companies and for Divisions of Large Companies.

In 1986, the Deming Committee established the Deming Application Award for Overseas Companies, which opened competition for the Deming Award to companies outside Japan. To date, the Florida Power and Light Company (FPL) is the only overseas company to receive this prize.

The Deming Award is granted by the Union of Japanese Scientists and Engineers (JUSE) to companies that successfully apply Total Quality Control (TQC) based on statistical quality control (SQC). JUSE was formed in 1946 as a non-profit-making body, to contribute to the development of culture and industry through the promotion of systematic studies for the advancement of science and technology. JUSE is the most influential organization in Japan for the development of the quality sciences and disciplines, and plays a major role in education and training, study missions and research projects.

Previous winners include Toyota, Komatsu, Yokogowa-Hewlett Packard, ASMO, Yuasa Batteries and many others.

Like the Baldrige Award, the Deming evaluation procedure commences with an application from the company in the preceding year. This consists of an outline of the company and a short summary of its Total Quality Control efforts. The second step involves a written examination, which requires an extensive compilation of the company's Total Quality Control efforts. This is known as the 'Descriptions of Quality Control (QC) Practices'. In a medium to large company this can run to hundreds if not thousands of pages of documentation.

Following a study of the written examination by the Committee, the third and final stage comprises an on-site examination. This comprises three elements:

1. Executives provide an introduction to their approach to TQC through presentations followed by unit demonstrations. These include videos, team presentations and tours of the workplace to demonstrate how Total Quality Control is being used in practice.
2. This section is led by the examiner and combines a brief overview of the department by its head followed by detailed questioning by the examiner. Included is a general session in which the unit has the opportunity to elaborate or to restate its approach to TQC, based on the questions asked.
3. The final stage comprises an executive session in which the examiners conduct a group interview with the executives to ask questions stemming from the executives views on Total Quality Control as written in the corporate description of Quality Control practices and to validate what the examiners learned during the examination.

As with the Baldrige Award the final evaluation is based on a scoring system with a maximum of 1,000 points. A maximum of 100 points is attainable in each category.

The Importance of Baldrige and Deming type awards

There can be no doubt that the existence of prestigious national and international awards are of major importance to the improvements in competitive performance. In the first two years following the establishment of the Baldrige Award its impact on US industry has been highly significant. In the words of Dr J.M. Juran:

'Let us start with the achievements reported during these two days by the Baldrige Award Companies. The reported results are stunning. The most visible feature of those achievements is their stunning magnitude. When our economists debate their forecasts of gains in national productivity, they are talking of a few per cent per year. The achieved gains of the Baldrige Award Winners have been far greater. Their reports include numerous cases in which during a few years:

- The time to provide customer service has been reduced by an order of magnitude

- Defect levels have been reduced by an order of magnitude
- Productivity has doubled
- Costs have been cut by 50 per cent.

The National Quality Award is a new force which has come over the horizon. In two short years it has grown in stature and in influence to a degree unprecedented in my experience in this field, and that dates back to 1924.

The award already has the potential to become the rallying point for US industry. For the first time since the quality crisis descended upon us, I have become optimistic. I now feel that we have a fighting chance to make enormous strides during the 1990s and once again to make 'Made in the USA' the symbol of World Class Quality.' (Summary address, 'The Quest for Excellence' an executive conference sponsored by the National Institute of Standards and Technology in conjunction with the American Society for Quality Control and the American Productivity and Quality Centre)

Quality in Europe

Due mainly to differences of history and language, the development of quality and its supportive institutionalization is markedly more fragmented in Europe than in either Japan or the United States.

The recognized European equivalent to the American ASQC and the Japanese JUSE is the European Organization for Quality (EOQ). This is an umbrella organization which recognizes as member bodies the National Institutions for Quality in each of the countries of Europe. The organization is not based on the EC but Europe as a continent, and has membership both in both eastern and western Europe. In the United Kingdom the official link to EOQ is through the British Quality Association (BQA). This organization comprises member firms in the United Kingdom. It shares a common Secretariat with the Institute of Quality Assurance which is open to individual membership. Similar arrangements, but with some variation, exist throughout continental Europe.

While there is currently no EC Quality body as such, there now exists a new organization within the EC, the European Foundation for Quality Management. This organization was formed in 1989 by a number of European companies concerned with the growing competition from outside. For much the same reasons as stated in the US Public Law 100–107 but as applied to Europe, the EFQM exists to promote Total Quality in member countries and organizations through the support of academic research activities, seminars, conferences and conventions. It is understood that the EFQM is currently studying the possibility of the promotion of a Quality award of similar status to the Deming and Baldrige Awards. Currently, it appears that the award will be called the European Award for Quality. Obviously, non-EC countries will share some concerns about this if the award is to be restricted to EC companies.

Within Europe there are currently a number of awards, both national and for individual endeavour. In the United Kingdom the BQA have a national prize known as the National Award for Quality, which has been growing in importance and prestige over the past few years. It is understood that this award is currently being reviewed in the light of the requirements for the Baldrige Award, with the likelihood that award criteria will be significantly developed. Other awards include the Institute of Administrative Management Quality Award, which was first awarded in 1990 to the Giro Bank in Liverpool.

Singapore: Total Quality – a national programme

Most people are aware of the impact of a national Quality strategy on Japan since World War II. Perhaps fewer westerners are aware that the same phenomenon is also occuring throughout the Far East, especially in Singapore.

In a typical Total Quality-style statement, Mr Lee Kuan Yew, the ex-Prime Minister of Singapore, said; Countries will have to compete to progress, whether or not they are part of a trade block.' This comment was made in an interview with Russell Skelton of News Limited and published in the *Weekend Australian*. Mr Lee went on to say: 'Phenomenally lower air and sea transportation costs mean that countries have to compete globally; should the Europeans become protectionist and exclude the Japanese and East Asians from their markets, they would be worse off in the medium term because of the lack of competition to spur them on to improve their products.' Multinational companies knew that to stay ahead in their fields, they would have to compete in the triad of America, Europe and the Asia–Pacific. He added that he believed the Asia–Pacific market would move from being the third to the second largest market within ten years. This attitude towards competition, growth and being the best in the world is the essence of Total Quality.

It is the mentality of being prepared to face all odds, to meet any challenge no matter how daunting it may seem, which is the essence of Total Quality and has enabled Singapore to gain its current success.

When Singapore was ejected from Malaysia in 1965, it was a run-down, Third World city, barely a country. The population consisted of Chinese, Malays and Indians, Christians, Moslems and a variety of other religions with virtually nothing in common, other than the fact that they all lived there. Hygiene was terrible, malaria rife, the water was undrinkable.

How has Singapore made such an incredible advance? Is it due to their geographic location? The population mix? Everyone in that part of the world puts it down to Lee Kuan Yew and his vision. Not everyone likes him. Not everyone necessarily agrees with his policies, or with their personal experiences living in what is often described as a sanitized environment. To achieve some of his goals he has introduced many penalties, usually in the form of fines: fines for dropping litter, for pestering to buy unwanted goods, for prostitution, for begging, speeding, for leaving stagnant water where mosquitoes can breed, etc. While the critics feel these impositions to be restrictive, almost all agree that the resultant disease-free society, absence of serious crime and the effective reduction of poverty is worth the restrictions. Furthermore, no one ever suggests an alternative means by which these successes might be achieved.

Conclusion

The key lessons to learn from Singapore are that the most incredible and unlikely achievements become attainable only when there is clarity of vision and the resolve against all odds to see them through. A defeatist attitude leads only to defeat. There is no reason other than lack of vision at the top why Great Britain or indeed any other European nation cannot equal or outpace the achievements of Japan, Singapore or any other industrialized country. Why is it that Nissan in Washington, Co. Durham, Sony in south Wales and all the other Japanese operating in the United Kingdom have equalled the performance of their parent companies in Japan even though they are employing British managers and British workers in a British environment? The only real difference is at the top management level. There is nothing that the Japanese manager does which cannot be emulated by his non-Japanese counterpart provided the will is there.

There are many other examples of British or other western

companies which lead to the same conclusion. Wedgwood and several others have been enormously successful with Quality Circles, a Total Quality concept. Just in Time (or Stockless Production as it should be known), which is one of the goals of Total Quality, has become one of the success stories of the late 1980s and early 1990s. There are numerous other examples, all of which indicate that success is achievable, and perhaps more importantly that had we not been so prepared to fall back so easily, our competitive position in the world could be much improved. We cannot rewrite the past, but we can influence the future. It is important to adopt a pro-active position. As Lee Kuan Yew said: countries will have to be competitive to progress. What are the implications for us if the concepts of Total Quality are to apply to national government?

Appendix III
Total Quality health check

Self-assessment inventory

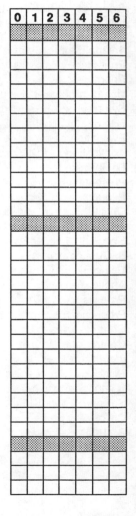

	0	1	2	3	4	5	6

1. Policy Management
Chairman's philosophy
Agreed corporate mission
Knowledge of market reputations
Knowledge of market share
Benchmarking
Knowledge of competitors' strengths/weaknesses
Knowledge of own strengths/weaknesses – market
Knowledge of own strengths/weaknesses – financial
Long-range/medium-range financial business plan
Key medium-range strategic success factors
Annual goals
Statistically-based annual goal measurement
2. Organization – Management
Deployment of goals structure
Line management mission statements
Deployed goals and targets – all levels
Performance feedback structure
Annual policy management audit and review system
Departmental audit and review system
Use of statistical methods at all levels
Performance recognition system
Project by project improvement teams
Quality Control Circles
Suggestion schemes
Facilitation/improvement programme support
Delegation of authority and terms of reference
Internal customer supplier improvement
3. Quality-related costs
Quality-related cost identification system
Key quality cost indicators
● Inventory finished goods

	0	1	2	3	4	5	6

- Inventory raw materials
- Inventory out of stock costs
- Work in progress
- Plant utilization – availability
- Labour utilization – efficiency
- Modification costs
- Yield
- Scrap/returns
- Rework/repeat performance
- Design/planning time effectiveness
- Customer complaint logging
- Customer complaint analysis
- Labour turnover costs including retraining

Use of statistical methods
Quality-related cost information dissemination

4. Quality improvement
Project identification
Prioritization
Use of problem-solving tools
Symptom – cause – remedy approach
Use of statistical tools
Evaluation of remedies
Application of PDCA cycle
Foolproofing
Presentation of results
Periodic audit of improvement
Quality Control Circle activities
Total preventive maintenance
Suggestion schemes

5. Quality control
Use of statistical Quality Control Techniques
Application of PDCA cycle
Process analysis
Process capability studies
Control of variables – use of control charts
Control of attributes – use of control charts
Identification of special causes
Dissemination of special causes to quality
   improvement process
Selection of measuring equipment
Calibration of measuring equipment

6. Quality assurance
New product development – organization
Use of market research information
Design review procedures
Involvement of internal functions

	0	1	2	3	4	5	6
Functional design reliability prediction and evaluation, life testing, FMEA							
Application of statistical methods							
Design for manufacture of operations							
PDCA cycle							
Process design, process analysis							
Product liability and risk analysis							
Organization of calibration and measurement control							
Audit and review programme – system							
Organization of quality control							
Subcontracting and purchasing control							
Subcontracting vendor rating							
Documentation							
Documentation on change control							
7. Education and training							
Education programme for all levels							
Quality consciousness							
Understanding of Total Quality programme							
Teaching of statistical concepts and dissemination							
Education of subcontractors, distributors and dealers							
Understanding project by project improvement process							
Understanding improvement techniques							
Understanding roles at all levels and own role							
Understanding and practising PDCA cycle							
Recognition of quality-related costs							
Understanding of QC Circle philosophy							
Understanding Total Quality philosophy							
Ability to make and implement improvement suggestions							
Confidence in presenting results							
Use of SQC software							
Education and training audit							
8. Standardization							
Standardization system							
Use of preferred numbers system							
Method of establishing, updating and superseding							
Control of internal standards							
Application of national and international standards							
Effectiveness of system to reduce cost and encourage best practice							

Suggested scoring method

For each parameter

0	Nonexistent
1	Vague – some evidence but very patchy
2	Vague – general awareness but not documented
3	Some documentation but unstructured
4	Documented but patchy use
5	Documented but only partially effective
6	Documented, used and effective

Radar chart

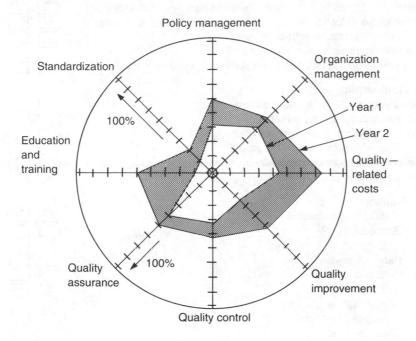

The diagram indicates the likely position of Company 'X' prior to commencement of Total Quality activities. This is indicated by the curve for year 1. After twelve months of development, the curve may look like that shown for year 2. If necessary, even the parameters used to bind the score can themselves be further broken down in greater detail. For example, an in-depth analysis of Quality Control Circle programmes may use a self-analysis programme such as the following:

Personal evaluation by QCC members

	Yes	No
1. Structure		
Is your involvement continuous?	☐	☐
Are QCC activities related to department goals?	☐	☐
Are the meetings regular?	☐	☐
Does the team always work on a project?	☐	☐
Are projects always completed?	☐	☐
Do you participate in presentations?	☐	☐
2. Enthusiasm		
Do you look forward to circle meetings?	☐	☐
Do QCC activities make you feel good?	☐	☐
Do you enjoy the company of other members?	☐	☐
Has participation made work more pleasurable?	☐	☐
Have circle activities improved relationships with management?	☐	☐
Have circle activities improved relationships with supervision?	☐	☐
Is there cooperation with other sections?	☐	☐
Do managers volunteer information?	☐	☐
Are you happy to risk making a daring suggestion?	☐	☐
3. Goal-setting		
Does your circle select its own projects?	☐	☐
Do you agree duties yourselves?	☐	☐
Do you organize your own activities?	☐	☐
Are your ideas listened to by group?	☐	☐
Do you set challenging goals?	☐	☐
Are projects in line with company goals?	☐	☐
4. Training		
Have you been trained in		
• Brainstorming?	☐	☐
• Data gathering?	☐	☐
• Pareto analysis?	☐	☐
• Histograms?	☐	☐
• Stratification?	☐	☐
• Concentration diagrams?	☐	☐
• Fishbone diagrams?	☐	☐
• Cause analysis?	☐	☐
• Paired comparisons?	☐	☐
• Presentation skills?	☐	☐
Do you know any other techniques?	☐	☐
Do you use techniques in projects?	☐	☐
Have you been trained in		
• Foolproofing?	☐	☐
• Control charts for variables?	☐	☐
• Control charts for attributes?	☐	☐
Can you identify quality-related costs in your area?	☐	☐

5. Support

Yes No

Do you have a facilitator?
Do you get the help you need?
Is the help just enough?
Do you make good use of management?
Do you cooperate with other circles?
Do managers attend presentations?
Does management implement circle suggestions?
If suggestions are not accepted are you told why?
Are non-circle colleagues cooperative?

6. Environment improvement

Are unions supportive?
Do you talk to your family about circles?
Is your family supportive?
Do non-circle members make suggestions?
Do you take an interest in other circles?
Are you kept informed about other companies' circles?
Do you see circle newsletters & notice boards?
Are you kept in touch with new techniques?
Do you know what the seven new tools are?

Again, the radar chart method may be used to indicate changes on an annual basis.

Total Quality health check

A full Total Quality health check includes both self-assessment and external assessment. These include:

- Customer surveys
- Opinion surveys (an example is included which forms part of a survey on QC Circle activities)
- Departmental audits
- Support material audits

The self-assessment element has been included here for the reader to form some opinion of the state of Total Quality within his or her own organization.

The radar chart is a useful method for plotting progress on an annual basis.

Details of the full health check can be obtained from:

David Hutchins Associates International Ltd
13/14 Hermitage Parade
High Street
Ascot
Berkshire
SL5 7HE

© David Hutchins Associates International Limited

Index